THE BOOK OF DAVID

A JOURNAL OF SUNSHINE, STORMS, RAINBOWS & MYSTERY

By

David V. Miller

To my special and favorite cousin and mentor, Bill Greif. I hope you enjoy this book.
David V. Miller
4-25-2016

Published by Blooming Ink Publishing, LLC

4712 East State Road 46
Bloomington, IN 47401

Copyright ©2015 by David Miller
Cover art Copyright © 2015 by David Miller
All Internal artwork is from public domain sites.

All rights reserved under Title 17, U.S. Code, International and Pan-American Copyright Conventions. No part of this work may be reproduced or transmitted in any form or by any means, electronic or mechanical, including but not limited to photocopying, scanning, recording, broadcast or live performance, or duplication by any information storage or retrieval system without prior written permission from the publisher, except for the inclusion of brief quotations with attribution in a review or report. To request permissions, please contact the author.

First Edition

ISBN: 978-1-943753-03-1

Table of Contents

Dedication 7
Acknowledgement 9
Introduction 13
I Wish 17
The Wisdom Of Four 21
Merry Christmas 25
Kids 29
Teens Who Compete 33
Veterans 37
About Seventeen-Year-Old Girls and Their Dads and Changes 43
A Rule to Live by – Peace in Silence 49
The Last Season 67
Summertime 71
A Christmas Lesson 75
The House at 923 State Street 85
    Dad 86
    Dad's Promotion 87
    Hello St. Joe 88
    Difficult Times 89
    The House 90
    Transformation 93
Male Basher 99
Civility 107
The Story of the Little Christmas Fox 111

The Story of Witch Hazel	117
It's All About Relationships	123
Happy Holidays	127
Being a Dad	133
The Party	137
Epilogue	**147**
Messages	149
To Hell and Back	153
My Train Wreck Graduates	159
Housebuilding – the Husband's Role	163
Children	169
Heroes	173
A Treasure from my Son	179
"Daddy"	**180**
What Has Happened To Us?	183
College Bound	189
A Question of Leadership	195
Times Have Changed	203
Prologue to a Matter of Bad Timing	209
A Matter of Bad Timing	211
Dad's Book	215
An Anniversary for Some Role Models	217
Moderation	221
Growing Old	225
Perfect Moment	229

Dog Walks	233
Bettye's Spirit	235
Mortality	239
Jack	243
Lonesome Pop	247
Beautiful Mother	253
Grieving For a Lost Daughter	259
Ashley's Graduation	261
Ashes	265
If I Could	269
Want a Job?	273
Human Connection (Einstein)	277
Sermons	281
I Will Probably Go to Hell for Saying this, but...	285
The Real Story of Adam and Eve	291
Two Views of the Universe	297
Galaxies	301
I. Questions	301
II. Credo	309
Love	318
ABOUT THE AUTHOR	323
ABOUT THIS BOOK	323

Dedication

Nothing that is perfect remains with us on this planet any longer than a few brief moments. A flawless sunset. A soft, bright rainbow. An aura of utter serenity. And you, Ashley Jane. Precious Ashley Jane. You, of the bluest eyes and soft, flowing auburn hair with its golden hue. You, Ashley Jane, a creature of pure beauty within and without. Vulnerable, demur, loving, gentle of mind and spirit, and, yes, perfect. You are one of God's angels, released from his presence like a sunset or a rainbow, to shine among us and upon us, a perfect star glowing here on the ground, warming every life you touched. But for a time too short, Ashley Jane. You could only remain with us for those few brief moments. Then God reclaimed you, as he does all of his sunsets, his rainbows, his auras of serenity . . . and yes, all of his angels. And on that day, Ashley Jane, God broke our hearts.

Acknowledgement

The Wind Beneath My Wings

I borrow the well-known lyrical phrase above to emphasize that embedded in this book are the inspiration, counsel, support and talents of some very special people. Here are their names and a short description of how and why our relationships and the fruits of their talents are ingredients of every page.

Max Ehrmann: I never met or spoke to Max Ehrmann, a lawyer and poet who lived most of his life in Terre Haute, Indiana. He died in 1945. However, Max Ehrmann speaks to me daily. I carry in my briefcase a hardback copy of Max's classic work of prose titled *"Desiderata."* I read it every day, sometimes more than once. In recent years, that has been the last thing I do before going to bed. *Desiderata* is a masterful reflection on our relationship with ourselves, our fellow humans, and our universe. In both form and substance, it is the most nearly perfect combination of words ever written in the English language. Those words provide the spiritual strength that sustains me and the fundamental perspective that gives context to every phase of my life. *Desiderata,* therefore, inspires the messages offered by this work.

Patti Knight Silke. I cannot imagine a friendship more complete than ours. For thirty-eight years Patti has assisted me in my work and has been wholly committed to my personal and professional best interests. I am equally committed to her welfare. I stood in for her deceased father at her wedding. Patti is my most adamant defender and most tactful critic. I trust her without condition. Never has any lawyer in the private practice been blessed with a more competent, loyal and talented assistant. She is my alter ego in professional affairs, she brings order to the chaos of my work, frees me from the minutia of my personal business affairs, and "she has my back." This book would not exist without her encouragement and hands-on help.

Launa Darnell Wakenhut. In January, 2015, I tracked Launa down through the internet and asked for her editorial help. We had not been in contact since May, 1965, when we were in our final days as undergraduates in the School of Journalism at the University of Michigan. We had become close friends in the autumn of 1963 while working together on journalism class assignments. I would critique her writing and she would critique mine.

Her writing was smooth and articulate, embellished by an enormous vocabulary. There was little to criticize. If a word was misspelled, in Launa's case, it was a typo. If I screwed something up, she was quick to catch it and tell me in the most tactful way.

Launa and I grieved together on November 22, 1963, as we stood at the AP wire machine and read the early reports of the murder of President Kennedy in Dallas. We shared a fellowship grant in 1964 that took us to Washington to report and provide commentary on the congressional debate of the Civil Rights Act of 1964. We saw one another almost every school day and had many discussions outside of class, mostly about the hot national issues of the day. Then I went off to law school in Indiana and Launa went....away....I did not know where she went. I have no memory of bidding her farewell in 1965, but surely we had a last moment and promised to keep in touch. And then 50 years passed in the blink of an eye, during which we had no contact at all.

In early 2015, I decided to write this book. Most writers have editors. I needed editors who would work for free. I thought just maybe Launa would help me again.....if I could find her. I assumed she had married and didn't know her husband's name. I was able to locate her, with the help of a paralegal assistant in my office. I am told it was pretty simple after she discovered that there was only one "Launa" in the U of M Class of 1965. So I sent Launa a message on Facebook. After a short period, I convinced her that I was who I claimed to be—her old college buddy who had failed to keep his promise to stay in touch. Launa immediately agreed to help with the editing, and she has done that and more.

It has been wonderful to have her help and even more of a pleasure to renew our friendship.

Elizabeth (Lisa) Delucio: I have the good fortune to have a law partner named Marco Delucio. He has the good fortune to have a wife named Lisa, who is a wife and mother first, and an artist with a love for the written word second. Lisa has been a vocal and persuasive supporter of my writings. She was one of the catalysts that pushed me to commit to this project. She promised to help review and edit my drafts, and she has contributed enormously in that respect.

And finally, there is my dad, Vincent Miller. He was my Number One Fan. He had, during his retirement, authored several autobiographical books himself. He personally printed and bound five copies of each – one copy for each of his four children and one copy for his own library. During one of our last visits together he said: "David, you have a gift. You are a writer. I will be very disappointed if you don't write a book. Write whatever you feel and think. Just open your brain and let your ideas come out." I promised him I would. His spirit has been with me every keystroke along the way.

Introduction

This book is about a little bit of everything human.

Parts of it are the result of periodically allowing my mind to wander and to wonder freely and off its leash. Sometimes the freed beast goes into the deepest recesses of my awareness. Other times, it remains in view, focused upon events occurring in the present. On occasion, I convert into words the images, thoughts, questions and the memories this process brings forth.

There are observations and stories about our common journey through life involving events warm and welcome, and events sad and painful. There are in every life seemingly mundane events that, in fact, are life-altering, moments that were "sweeter than we knew" and times when the uncontrolled, often brutal, role of Fate snatches those moments from us without warning or apology.

There are fundamental mysteries that accompany each of us from cradle to grave—mysteries that give birth to vexing questions. If we knew the answers, we may not like them but, nevertheless, the questions deserve to be asked and discussed. Some of that occurs in these pages.

There is no required beginning or end to this book. The first section could have been anywhere else in the sequence. In some respects, that reflects the randomness of the circumstances, challenges and individuals that we all encounter daily. At the same time, it is a recognition and appreciation of the variety and potential that abounds in the human race and the often unseen but heavy burdens we individually bear.

Human experiences form the springboard from which we develop wisdom—or not. Some of these pages explore the most basic differences between wisdom and knowledge.

Here is the reality: There is no guarantee of fairness associated with this existence. In fact, there are no guarantees at all. The strongest hearts can be broken, the strongest wills can prevail, or not, against heavy odds, and acts of kindness and lives of integrity often go unrewarded. Yet despite all of the challenges and injustice and mysteries and natural disasters and baseless intolerance that permeate human history and even our current circumstances, the pesky, intrepid human race not only survives, but flourishes.

Our race arose on this planet in the most difficult of living conditions and with a completely empty slate of scientific knowledge. Moreover, we, as a species, have consistently bungled the management of our common affairs. Nevertheless, we have done amazingly well in sorting out some of the essential governmental, philosophical and physical questions without any playbook. However, we still have a very long way to go on all of those fronts. We continue to differentiate ourselves by establishing borders and religious sects. Consequently, violence and war seem endless.

At an individual level though, we have done better. We have learned that it is okay to laugh and it is okay to cry. It is okay to celebrate and it is okay to grieve. It is okay to ask questions that cannot be answered with certainty and to seek that certainty. It is okay to learn, succeed, fail and excel. It is okay to help a stranger in need and it is okay to be that stranger. It is okay to be weak and okay to be strong. It is okay to love whomever we choose and it is okay to be who and what we are. Most important of all, it is okay for each one of us to understand that we have a right to be here and that we have, in turn, the responsibility to respect that right in others.

This is our one and only time to live. It is not easy, it is not always fair. It ends badly. But while we are here, we should remember every day that life is a gift that is best used to make pleasant memories and to learn as much as we can about our place in this universe. Because this is as good as it gets.

<u>I Wish</u>

S OMETIMES I wish the world could be like it was in my childhood when it was filled with good people and everyone's door was unlocked and all the customers on my paper route were my friends and complete security was only as far away as my mom and baseball was the most important thing except for football and basketball depending on the time of year it was and nobody I loved died and I didn't worry about anything and my family always had an evening meal together and we called that meal "supper" and I believed in Santa Claus until I was 10 and my mom was embarrassed about that so she told me and I was disappointed and then I turned 11 and I sold ice cream at Bosse Field every summer night when the Braves were in town and I got in for free and earned about a dollar and I could walk home from there at 10 p.m. and not be afraid and my mom didn't have to worry that some bad person would hurt me on the way and people burned their leaves in the Fall and that made it smell good and I didn't know what "politics" meant and Notre Dame won all the football games and we had a drug store with a soda fountain and fresh ice cream right on the corner and mom would send me to the grocery store on the other corner to get a loaf of fresh white bread for 17 cents and the milkman brought our milk right to the door and the mailman's name was Clarence and there was no air conditioning but everybody had electric fans and sat out on their porches on hot summer nights and popsicles were a nickel at the drug store and there were enough kids on my block so that there was always somebody to play with and they were always nice to me except when they weren't and then I would tell my mom and she would make me feel better and nobody had a TV so people would come around and visit and stay a while and I would read about Mickey, Willie and Duke and Stan on the sports page of the newspaper and donuts also cost a nickel and hamburgers were usually a dime and lots of people walked to work every morning and I walked to St. Anthony School and Sister Joseph Ann loved me and we only had one car and it was old but that was okay because we didn't travel out of town very often and if we did we didn't go very far and I had so many cousins and aunts and uncles I couldn't count 'em all but I knew all their names and they all loved me too and I could ride my bike to all their houses except one that was on a busy highway and my aunts would always feed me and be glad to see me when I showed up there and they would call my mom on our party-line phone and tell her I was there and then they would talk for hours and every year I would get really nice hand-me-down clothes for free that my older cousins had outgrown and I would go with my mom to shop on Main Street on Friday nights because that's when Dad got paid and she would put things on layaway that she really wanted and pay a dollar a week until she paid the whole price and then we would meet Dad and some friends or aunts and uncles and cousins at the K of C for dinner and Dad would drink too many beers sometimes and we all went to Mass together on Sundays and sometimes I would misbehave and be in trouble but not for very long and then we would go visit my grandparents who lived in this little bitty house on the west side where my dad grew up and my grandma would give me anything I wanted. That's what I wish sometimes.

But to have the heart of a child is not a disgrace. It is an honor. A man must comport himself as a man... But it is never a reproach that he has kept a child's heart, a child's honesty and a child's freshness and nobility.
– Ernest Hemingway, *True At First Light: A Fictional Memoir (1999)*

The Wisdom Of Four

THE BEST AGE TO BE IS FOUR. When you are four, you are mobile, potty trained, cute, able to communicate and you are not required to go to school.

There is no pretense in the words or actions of a four-year-old. And at four, nothing is held back. When you're happy, you laugh. When you're sad, you cry. When everything's okay, you play and be loud or watch T.V. When you're tired, you gripe and moan and misbehave and be generally loud until some big person gives you a warm bath, hugs you for a while and sings to you for a while and you go to sleep wherever. And the next morning you start all over again. Nobody is mad at you about what you did or said yesterday, even if it was really horrible. You always get more chances to be loved when you're four. And there are no competitive sports or music lessons to stress you out when you are four.

Except for the video tapes, that's what being four was like at my house when I was a little person, and that's what being four has been like at my house now that I'm a big person. I am also satisfied now that God wants four-year-olds to be loud most of the time. So they are.

Four-year-olds think pretty hard about the things they see and hear, and most of them have their own uncomplicated view of the world. Here are some of the rules of life for four-year-olds I've known well:
- If you are tired, you can go to sleep no matter where you are.
- If you want someone to hold you, say so, and someone will.
- If you don't like somebody, there is a good reason and you don't have to hang around with that person, and you don't have to worry about it.
- Nobody but Mom and Dad can be your boss unless you let them.
- You are still too young to have chores.
- You only have to grow up if you want to.
- Every big person's job is just as important as every other big person's job.
- A person only ever needs to find one job.
- Mommy and Daddy can fix anything that is wrong.
- Learning is fun.
- Getting money is easy and it can be found at the place Dad works.
- Grandmothers will give you anything you want.
- If you're not having fun with a friend, you find another one.
- There is almost no problem in the world that cannot be solved with a hug.

- The best place to be when things are stormy is very close to the people who care the most about you.
- Love is free.
- You have fun and laugh every day.
- When someone who loves you gets mad at you, it doesn't mean that person doesn't love you anymore.
- Hitting is absolutely wrong unless somebody hits you first.
- People who are grown up should never hurt people who are not grown up, ever.
- Santa Claus is real and so are Mickey Mouse and Sesame Street.
- If you choose to irritate an older brother or sister, he or she might forget one of the rules about hitting.
- Once you've told a lie, you can't take it back.

It should come as no surprise that four-year-old children can be wiser than adults. Their minds aren't burdened with the pretense and cunning and prejudice that afflict many adults. Too bad the world of adults is not governed by the wisdom they learned when they were four. It would be a safer and more serene place to live. But since that will never happen, I'm just going to hang out with as many four-year-olds as I can. You can come along if you want.

Merry Christmas

THE HOUSE I LIVED IN when I was a child was a solid old late Victorian place where my mom and eight siblings had grown up. It had high ceilings and wide archways between the living room and dining room on the main floor. The living room had a fireplace. It was a perfect place for the magic of Christmas to unfold. And my parents worked hard to make that happen.

A few days before Christmas, my dad would use tacks to place a big blanket across the doorway leading from the dining room into the living room. I would watch him put it up. When dad was finished, the living room was off limits. He said nobody, not even adults, could go into that room until after Santa had been there on Christmas Eve.

When the blanket went up, the living room contained no sign of Christmas. No decorations, no tree, no candles, no gifts – nothing. I didn't know it then, but my dad waited until the very last minute to buy our Christmas tree. In fact, I didn't know our Christmas tree was bought at all. I thought it magically appeared and Santa decorated it when he brought the gifts. There was a never-used doorway into the living room from our front porch. Mom and Dad always said it was "nailed shut." I didn't know it then, but that door was never nailed shut. It was locked and my Dad had the only key. And I know now that the only time that door was ever used was when the blanket was up and I was asleep or away from the house.

As Christmas Eve approached, the excitement was almost too much for a young heart to stand. My attention would be diverted by helping mom bake cookies, and visits from cousins and sledding excursions with dad. But never for a moment could I forget that very soon Santa would somehow magically turn my living room into a Christmas paradise full of gifts and decorations in an instant when I wasn't looking. And I was almost always looking.

At every chance, I would sneak toward the front of the house, especially on Christmas Eve Day, and I would lay down on the floor of the dining room at the door into the living room and peer under that blanket. But the blinds were closed and the lights were off and it was too dark in there for me to see anything. A few times, I was caught by mom or dad while I was sneaking a peek under that blanket. They would say it was risky for me to peek – that if Santa had been there when I peeked, he would go on to the next house and not come back. And I believed them. But sometimes, I just couldn't help it. I didn't know it then, but they knew I couldn't help it. In fact, they would have been disappointed if I had not peeked.

Christmas Eve afternoon was a busy time every year. Until I was nine years old, which is when I discovered the awful truth, I was always somewhere away from the house during that time. It just seemed that something always came up. I didn't know it then, but there was a lot of magic going on in that living room during that time when I was away, and Santa didn't have anything to do with it.

Darkness fell early on Christmas Eve, just as it does now. The late afternoon and dinner hour were filled with the sounds of Christmas music from the radio, but every minute seemed like a year. That time was occupied with baths and getting dressed for midnight mass and grandparents arriving, and dinner in the kitchen; and all the while I could not understand how the adults could be so calm. Didn't they understand what was about to happen here? Didn't they know that Santa could be in that living room at that very moment? And how could they eat dinner at a time like this?

At long last, I would be excused from the dinner table – no child ever left the dinner table in those days without being excused – and I would peek around the corner at the blanket. And, like magic, the blanket would be gone, the fireplace would be ablaze, the light from the Christmas Tree would be shining out into the rest of the house, and suddenly Christmas would consume me.

It wasn't the gifts I unwrapped that were memorable on those nights. I don't recall a single one. It was the wonder and the magic and the unconditional love that filled that house on those nights. That is what I remember and treasure. I didn't know it then, but I know now, that those were the real gifts my parents were giving to me during those special Christmas seasons. The gifts of wonder and magic and love at Christmas.

I thought you might like to know it, too. Maybe there are some kids in your life who still know Santa and maybe you can give them the same gifts. If you do, I promise that you and they will have a memory to keep and a very Merry Christmas.

<u>Kids</u>

MY MIND has been on kids a lot lately. At least I thought I was thinking about kids, but I really wasn't. I was thinking about the behavior and troubles that American kids display and cause, and I was wondering: What on earth has happened here? I've seen on the ten o'clock news or heard about it on NPR or read about it in the newspaper. What I see and hear and read tells me that a large number of American adults are doing a very poor job of taking care of an even larger number of American kids.

I heard a story on the local news recently about an 11 year old boy who was hunted down and sodomized by three other boys. One of the bullies was 12. The other two haven't been caught yet, but they're not very old either — maybe 14. Those of you who can, think back thirty years and try to imagine that kind of news story. Or try to imagine a group of kids pushing a nine year old boy out of a tenth floor window so he wouldn't rat on them. Something has gone seriously wrong here. Or try to imagine taking a loaded gun to school just to feel safe. It could be that these events are unavoidable. That all of the parents and caretakers of the kids who do these things did all that was possible to love and nurture and discipline and protect them. But I don't think so.

As a society, when it comes to taking the time and making the sacrifices necessary to treat our kids the way we would want to be treated, the way most of us WERE treated when we were kids ourselves, a huge number of American parents don't measure up. We don't even come close, and the ways our kids misbehave reflects it.

You don't believe me? Ask the teachers — the ones who have been around for a while. I know a preschool teacher who has been at it for over 20 years. She's one of the best. She loved her job and she was a godsend to her students. She's ready to quit. Kids who are three and four years old curse at her and defy her and disrupt her class every day. And these are kids from "good" homes. In this case, "good" is translated as "high income." Obviously, earning a lot of money doesn't assure that a kid's behavior will be acceptable. Money can't buy that.

Family economics aside, many of us are failing our kids and, therefore, ourselves, in every aspect of child-rearing. It is happening right in front of our eyes. How many of you have been too afraid to confront a group of teens acting in a totally unacceptable way in a public place? I'm not talking moral matters, I'm talking about kids, whether in groups or not, answering to no one, breaking the law, intimidating and threatening others, driving cars, trucks and motorcycles in a way that creates real danger.

How many of you have watched a parent close his or her eyes, helpless or unwilling to stop the obvious revolting or lawless behavior of a small child? Was it too much trouble to deal with? Was the parent afraid of the child? Or too embarrassed? Were mom and dad just too tired, or did they close their eyes, resigned to the inevitable? Whatever the excuse, there is no excuse. We fail our children, ourselves and our world when we let this happen.

The problem is not economic, it is systemic. We are too busy making money, or doing our own thing, or making ends meet, or finding ourselves, or making our marks, or doing it all. We are selfish, much more so than our parents and theirs. Many of us define what we think are our own material "needs," and our personal career goals and our desire for self-fulfillment and public esteem. And we use all of our energy to get there. All of it. Then we give our kids what is left — which is either nothing or not very much.

On top of that, there are the many people who regard parenting as a burden instead of a privilege. I wish I could count the number of times I've heard someone say how glad they will be when their kids are grown and gone. Bad attitude. And almost without fail, their kids reflect that attitude in misbehavior, disrespect, irresponsibility and lack of ambition.

Everyone who does so has an excuse for putting the kids second, or third, or worse. Whatever the excuse, the results are the same. When children do not get the love and care and discipline they crave, they feel rejected and cheated and they strike back. They are the angry children who are alone, lost, defiant, mean, dangerous, or poor students, or all of the above. So they find ways to get attention — the wrong ways.

We need to wake up. We need to regain control. It's not that hard to figure out. Somebody needs to love the kids and to be there for them all the time, every day. No excuses. Their need for care and love and discipline must come first, all the time, every day. Somebody who loves them and who they respect and love has to impose discipline and make it stick. Somebody they respect and who sets a decent example has to tell them: "This is right, that is wrong, and this is why." We have to treat our kids from womb to emancipation like special gifts from God to be savored and enjoyed, not like curses or burdens to be endured or cast adrift. Someone needs to hug every kid every morning and every night and really mean it. And if you don't mean it, don't bother; kids can tell the difference.

It's okay to get tired. It's okay to get angry. It's okay to despair and to wonder where the money will come from to pay everything you must pay. It's okay to cry and feel like you're entitled to some relief. You are, and you should get it. And it's okay to need help and to ask for it and to accept it. But it's not okay to quit, and it's not okay to put yourself before your kids. And it's not okay to let the kids run wild because you just don't care or because it's too much trouble. The unacceptable results of irresponsible parenting are all around us.

Teens Who Compete

I'VE WATCHED SEVERAL GROUPS of responsible teenagers grow up together who compete in various sports. It's been one of the great pleasures of my life. The teens I've watched most recently were mostly 15 and 16 years old when I realized the significance of what I am about to say. They are representative of teenage athletes everywhere, both boys and girls.

They've known one another, competed with and against one another and loved the same sports for most of their lives. They've grown together, worked together and known victory and defeat together. As time passed, their dedication to their games and their determination to perform to the best of their abilities sealed their friendships. So today, whether they are on the same team or on different teams, they are one.

They are works in process – on the short side of adulthood, just discovering life's promises and burdens. They are feeling their way toward adulthood and wondering where it all leads. But they are defined by their self-discipline, their work ethic, their dedication to excellence and to one another and to the sports they love.

However, the more important message, and the best news, is this. There are teenagers like this, all around us. They are in every neighborhood and in every school, from east coast to west.

And they are more than just athletes. They are students with ambitions and talents. They are musicians, debaters, thespians and artists. They are interested in writing, science, math, politics and, yes, socializing. They are in school every day chasing their potential, and wondering what it is and where they will find it. They help to define what is good and wholesome in their schools and towns. They are leaders without the need of titles.

Kids like this work a kind of double shift to compete in the sports they love and at the same time obtain the education that will define their future. So they are not, like so many big-time college jocks, just athletes who happen to be enrolled in school. They are student-athletes in the purest sense.

The added responsibility they bear is heavy. When 15 to 25 after-school hours are consumed by practices and competitive matches every week, the body rebels against homework and deadlines and studying for exams. But they know they serve both masters, because if they don't, they can't play or compete. And if they can't play or compete, they will be miserable and let themselves and their teammates down. So they give up their time at the mall, fight the rebellion and meet the challenge. They practice for hours and then do their homework, get their rest and use whatever time is left, which isn't much, to hang out.

They are, all of them, wherever they live, so focused on their responsibilities at school, and so involved in training, practicing and playing their games that they have neither the time nor the inclination to make the front page by misbehavior. Their drugs of choice are camaraderie, achievement and competition; and their conduct of choice is to play by the rules.

Yes, their bedrooms can resemble train wrecks. Yes, they are moody. Yes, they still require care and supervision and discipline. And yes, they sometimes make mistakes. But they are, in most cases, pretty responsible teens who are a pleasure to be around. They are a big part of the promise of our future; and they make parenting a joy.

It really doesn't matter what sports they choose or where they live or go to school. What matters is that they are out there, everywhere, and that they are dedicated to their goals. What matters is that they know the price of success because they pay it every day.

They know that winning is fun and important, and that losing can be overcome. They know that they can't win anything alone, that the credit for winning and the blame for losing is properly shared with coaches and teammates. They know that it's okay to depend on others for help, and that everyone should encourage their buddies to excel. They know how to be friends. They know what loyalty and determination and personal responsibility are all about.

And maybe most important of all is this. They know the rules. That's important because, when you think about it, the rules for living and the rules for athletic competitions are basically the same: Work hard, play hard, stay in bounds and don't cheat. Most teenage athletes follow those rules at school, at home and when they compete. That's why they don't make the front page. And that's why we can count on them when it's their turn to help run this place.

<u>Veterans</u>

The Press
Friday, April 11, 1997

FOR MOST of the year, the chief veteran lives in the concession stand at the Little League field nearby. He's happy these days. He's watching the field come to life after the long silence of winter. The chief veteran has probably been at that ball park every day that anyone has been there since the field has been there. He's there for sign-ups, tryouts, practices, everything. He grooms the field, he talks sports with his co-veteran buddies, he gets to know young athletes and he watches kids play baseball whenever and wherever he can.

He's been the coach of the team with the gold uniforms for about thirty years. But the only time he plays favorites is during his own team's games. He loves baseball, kids who play baseball, baseball fields and anyone who cares about any of the above. He loves concession stands at baseball fields where he can hang out. And he does hang out there, even during the off season and on rainy days. He loves his co-veteran buddies too, who love all of the same things he loves. He also loves his cigarettes, but he keeps them and his smoke away from the kids. He can be forgiven one vice for all the good he's done.

The chief veteran and his buddies have watched, worked, and taught the game and sportsmanship for a long,

long time – just for the fun of it. During that time, kids named Griese, Mattingly, Schultz, Henning, Brownlee, Merkel, Gries, MacCauley, Benes and thousands of others played, learned, won and lost and grew to manhood right before their eyes. They watch and work and teach still today. And still today, they have a great time doing it. The concession stand is their clubhouse, the ball field is their golf course, and they would be lost at sea without them. So would thousands of kids.

There is a chief veteran and a group of co-veterans at every youth sports facility I've ever been to – and I have been to about a million. It's about time we recognize how much the whole community benefits from their presence.

Not too long ago, when the veteran and I were growing up, there weren't many opportunities for kids who wanted to play organized sports. There were a few Little League baseball teams, and some grade school teams for basketball and football. But that was it.

Most of us back then learned our sports skills and rules in empty schoolyards or in alleys where someone had hung a basketball goal. There were no veterans around to help us, and it showed when we played. Even if we did make a team, we played poorly, the seasons were short, and there weren't many practices.

I can remember dreaming of the day when I'd be old enough to try out for a real Little League team. You had to be nine. All the rules I knew until then were the neighborhood rules. Those rules did not always comport with the official rules. So there I was at tryouts, assuming the neighborhood rules applied. When it came my turn to bat, I let the first pitch go by. The man behind the plate said, "Strike!" I was confused. I hadn't even swung, much less missed. What was wrong with this guy? You had to swing and miss or foul it off. Otherwise, it was a "Ball." Didn't he know that? By the time I figured out that if you let a decent pitch go by it was a Strike, I was already out. I didn't make the team.

A lot of kids got left out in those days. Girls were left out entirely. They couldn't even try out and screw up like me. They were girls, so they were out. It was a bad system. It was, in fact, no system at all.

Time and a couple of generations of parents have changed all that. The boys who got to play back then, and some of the boys and girls who didn't, became those parents. And now, they're the veterans. They were baby boomers who wanted to see their kids and other kids play and compete and learn. So all over the country they spent their evenings, their Saturdays and their money creating a huge diversity of youth sports programs and facilities for every age and competitive level.

Today, if a kid is potty trained and wants to play a sport, there's a team somewhere nearby to play on. Name the sport: baseball, basketball, football, soccer, hockey, volleyball, tennis, swimming, gymnastics, golf, motocross. The list is endless, the seasons are longer, practices are serious business, and the competition is not just local. The result is a new generation of healthier kids who learn physical endurance, have great fun and grow stronger in mind and body. It took a lot of years and a lot of people like the chief veteran and his co-veterans to make all this happen. But it has.

The system isn't perfect. There are some poor coaches. There are some parents whose behavior is an irritation and embarrassment to their own children and to everyone else. In some places, cliques and politics dominate. All that's too bad, but it's outweighed a hundredfold by the lessons, the opportunities and the memories these leagues give to the kids who play the games.

It's the veterans who make it all work. They're the ones who have coached so long, raised money so long, worked on the fields and gone to meetings so long, and done all of the thankless work of youth sports so long that the rest of us believe they live in the concession stands. Some of their spouses believe it too. The spouses think it's either that, or they're having affairs. In fact, they are having affairs. They're in love with the innocence and the promise of youth sports. And they're determined to preserve that innocence and promise.

So no matter what the sport, the next time you pass a ball park or a playing field and you see a game going on, or the next time you see a veteran touching young lives at a practice or in an arena, think for a minute. Think about the remembered lessons and the impossible heroics they're creating. Think about the purity and innocence of youth sports. Think about all the work and love and fun it took to make happen what you just saw happen. And the next time you see the chief veteran or any veteran at any of those ball parks, fields or arenas, tell 'em, "Thanks."

About Seventeen-Year-Old Girls and Their Dads and Changes

Published Friday, September 1, 1995, *The Evansville Courier*
Republished Wednesday, December 5, 2007, *Evansville Courier &Press*

THERE HAVE been train wrecks neater than this child's room. She is 17. Seventeen is a tough age for a dad. Not his age – hers. Girls are different now than they were when I was 17.

When I was 17 girls were dancers and cheerleaders and singers and they played the piano and they dressed really perfect. Not a hair out of place. Tons of hair spray made sure of that.

I never got into a girl's room when I was 17, but those who did tell me that is the only thing about 17-year-old girls that has not changed about 17-year-old girls since I was 17.

True enough, there are still some girls who lead cheers and some who dance or sing or play the piano, but even those girls are different. When they're not dancing or cheering or playing the piano, and even sometimes when they do, they are wearing baseball caps and T-shirts with political or social messages. Messages such as . . . well, never mind. And my 17-year-old, who, by the way, does not dance (anymore) or lead cheers (anymore) or play the piano (anymore), very often wears cleats. A lot of her friends do too.

When I was 17, girls did not wear cleats. They had no reason to wear cleats. Cheerleading and dancing and singing and piano playing did not require cleats. Cleats, of course, are for running and cutting in athletic endeavors. Every girl I knew when I was 17 only walked. Not one of them ran – ever. Walking does not require cleats, either.

Along with her cleats, my 17-year-old girl wears athletic shorts that read "Umbro" and shirts with numbers on the back and athletic bras. When I was 17, shirts with numbers only fit boys, and girls only wore shorts to stay cool when it was hot. And, as far as I knew, athletic bras did not exist. And girls didn't need shirts with numbers on the back because cheerleaders and dancers and singers and piano players didn't have numbers. Ballplayers had numbers.

When I was 17, girls didn't play in ballgames; they watched ball games. That, of course, is no longer true, and I am happy about that. Sometime between my 17th birthday and now (did I say "NOW"?), the lives of 17-year-old girls have changed a lot.

In most respects, the benefits of that change are beyond dispute, although I don't necessarily think all of those changes have been good for the girls or for our world. We are paying heavy social prices for many of them.

But social prices were being paid for centuries by the women who did not have the benefit of this revolution.

Remember, for instance, that when I was 17, nobody even bothered to teach girls to run or to remain fit or to play ball. Conditioning and sports were only for boys.

On Saturday, I went to the local high school soccer jamboree.

That's another change from when I was 17. There was no high school soccer then, for boys or girls.

I feel cheated by that myself. But that's another issue. Or is it?

Anyway, there I was, at the soccer jamboree, and I was watching and cheering for my team, a team of girls.

One of the girls on the team was my 17-year-old who wears baseball caps, T-shirts with political and social messages, and all manner of unappealing clothing.

She finds the clothing she wears by digging through layers of debris in her room.

The differences in the way boys and girls play the same games are not important. Athletic games teach endurance, dedication, body awareness, self-discipline, how to win, how to lose, how to be a team player, how to have fun, and other lessons about life.

Lifetime friendships are born on athletic fields.

It was long past due that all children should have those same benefits.

For a long time I thought my 17-year-old didn't know how lucky she is that she got to be 17 in 1995 instead of 1955. Then one day last year as I was climbing through the rubble in her room, I saw a page she had torn from a magazine and taped onto her wall. It was a full-page ad for women's athletic wear. It had a drawing of a girl playing soccer, running hard in the middle of the page. The girl's hair was flying behind her and these words were on the page above and below her:

> When you were a child your mother thought,
> As mothers sometimes do,
> That you were strong enough
> And sure enough
> To someday be a dancer.
> But When you were five or was it six or was it nine
> You didn't want to dance, you couldn't bear to dance
> Unless you were dancing in the grass,
> And dancing in the mud
> As children often do
> As children often do.
>
> And then your father kicked to you a ball.
> And the ball was the shape of the whole wide world to you.
> And now if you see green you can only think of one thing to do.
> And the world slips away from your feet.
> And the sky slips down into your arms.
> And you are free you are free you are absolutely free

To be who you want. To go where you can.
To be wild to be loud to fly in the mud and run in the rain.
Strong enough.
And sure enough.
Like a dancer.

That message was an almost exact reflection of her own experience. It is still on her wall today. When I was finished reading it, there was a lump in my throat. And I didn't care about the mess in her room anymore.

Some things just aren't that important and don't need to change.

Some things do.

A large number of the guys who were 17 when I was 17 sometimes struggle with all the changes.

But we'll get by.

A Rule to Live by – Peace in Silence

FROM "FATE," there is no place to hide. Fate is the unforeseeable over which we have no control. Fate plays no favorites among the innocent and the not-so-innocent. Fate can turn the peace and order of one moment into chaos, uncertainty or tragedy in the next. Fate transforms dreamers into icons, and turns icons into has-beens.

Fate, sometimes temporarily and sometimes permanently, turns lives upside down, interrupts plans, teaches lessons and even creates opportunities. Fate has no governor, makes no apologies and takes no credit. We are ever vulnerable to its whims. Some things just happen.

Fate visits life and death crises upon people of all ages. It places challenges that seem unsolvable in our path. And it can provide solutions when none appears possible. Fate is the mother of the adage that life carries with it no guaranty of fairness.

During the early 1950s, Fate entered the life of my friend, Robert, when he was only sixteen and growing awkwardly toward manhood in a small town in Tennessee. Robert and I became friends many years later while working together.

One evening, during a casual dinner, Robert told me of a crisis he had faced alone during his second year in high school. He had experienced Fate at work on several levels at once. He regarded those few days as the most dangerous and the most instructive growing experience of his life. They were dangerous because if the crisis had not been resolved skillfully, violence aimed at him and his family would have followed. They were "instructive" because, at the very moment when he was most alone and unsure of what to do, he had chanced upon a few words of advice from an unlikely source. It suggests that even though Fate has no governor, at least in some circumstances it has a fulcrum.

This is Robert's story of his encounter with Fate.

****

Andrew Jackson High School fielded a very good football team that season. I can say I was a "member" of that team. "Member" is the only word I can think of, and even that might give my role a tad too much credit. To put it another way, the team was undefeated during the 10-game season, winning by an average of about 40 points per game, and I was present at every practice.

Memories dim with time, but I recall being permitted to put on an official uniform and sit on the official home team bench for one game. I was so low on the roster that my name did not appear in any game program all season.

The head coach was a beloved football legend in our town. He was a foul-mouthed but kind product of the Great Depression and WWII who had returned from fighting in the Pacific to play halfback on a UT team that had gone to a bowl game on New Year's Day. He lived football and he loved all of his players as if we were his own sons, even me. And he was a disciplinarian, a man of complete honor who tolerated no rule breaking by any player. He had once kicked a star quarterback off the team just for saying something disrespectful about the mother of another player.

The only distinction I had on the team was my nickname. The assistant coach, on the first day of practice, labeled me "Bones" because he said that's what I looked like – a small stack of bones. The label stuck with me for the rest of my high school days. I'd bet at least half of the students in my class didn't know my name was Robert until it was pronounced on graduation day.

But even before that first day of practice, just like the head coach did, I knew all the players' names. I admired them, especially the "starters," in the way I should have admired the war-hero head coach.

That's what I called them, "starters." I would go far out of my way between classes just to invite a smile or a nod of the head from any one of them.

I am now certain that the coaches kept me off the playing field that year because they thought I was so loosely assembled by my Creator that I might be badly injured if they put me in a real game. At the beginning of the first year of high school, I was only about 5 feet 6 inches tall and I weighed about 130 pounds. By the end of that school year, I had shot up to 6 feet 2 inches but I still weighed only 140 pounds. That fast eight-inch growth spurt made me one of the clumsiest humans on the planet. I could barely walk without stumbling or bumping into a person or a wall. Skinny and clumsy. That's what I was. And "Bones" was who I was.

    I would have been no match for most of the players from the other teams. Almost all of them were more physically mature and much bigger and faster than I was. By the time I would have been subbed into a game, the other teams' players would be embarrassed and madder than hornets because of the score was so lopsided. They would have loved to have me as a target late in those games.

    Now here is the predicament that I, "Bones," found myself in soon after the school year began.

    I owed my parents $50. That's how much I had borrowed from my dad that previous summer to buy my first car. Man, you should have seen that car. It was so cool – a 1950 two-door Ford that, at one time, had been blue. It wasn't exactly blue anymore but mostly you could tell it used to be. And, anyway, what color a car is or isn't doesn't affect how it runs. And "Ol Blue" ran pretty good most of the time except when it was real cold outside.

So, to earn the money I needed to pay off the $50, I took a second job at the high school as one of the cashiers at the end of the cafeteria line in the school lunch room. My other job was a morning newspaper route.

The cafeteria cashier job was pretty cushy. I was released early from the last class before the lunch period. I would go directly to the cafeteria and there would be a lunch tray with items totaling fifty cents in value waiting for me. My lunch items were chosen by the lady who ran the cafeteria. Fifty cents would buy plenty of food, even for a hungry, growing teenage boy in those days. Hamburgers were a dime, a plate lunch with two vegetables and bread was 25 cents and milk was a nickel. I would take my food to the cashier's station and eat quickly before the onslaught of students came through the cafeteria line.

There were two food lines and two cashiers. The students would slide their trays on the rails along one side or the other of the food selections and bring their filled trays to the exit gates where the cashiers sat. We would add up the cost of the items on a tray, collect what was owed from the student and put the money in the cash box. That was how it worked. No cash registers, no records, no adding machines, no security cameras – life was simple. The "cash box" I used was a small container designed to hold fishing lures and hooks.

This job, I thought, was going to make it easy for me to pay my $50 debt. I would save the entire $2.50 in lunch money my mom gave me at the beginning of every school week. The lunch money, along with my paper route money, went into a cigar box that I kept under my bed. That was the source of the money I had to buy gas for my car and to take my girlfriend on dates. Gas was 20 cents a gallon. One dollar would buy a week's supply of gas. I figured I could pay about $2 every week on the loan and pay it off by the next spring.

Then, a couple of weeks after school started, my neat little financial plan came crashing down. One fine Thursday, as I sat at the cashier's station doing my noontime job, a very large senior who was a starter on the football team came through with a loaded tray of food. As he approached, I greeted him and began adding up the charges for all the items on the tray. He owed well over a dollar, but I couldn't finish adding what he owed because he just kept walking. He didn't speak to me but he smiled and put a quarter on the counter as he went by. I didn't know him well, but I knew he had just stolen at least a dollar's worth of food and I knew he was a big dude. He took his lunch to a table where some other senior football players were sitting.

I couldn't leave the cashier station, but I was stunned and immediately confused about what to do. The line of students continued, so I could do nothing immediately except carry on with my work. When the student traffic subsided, it was time to go to the next class. I was afraid of the guy who took the food, and afraid of some of his buddies at his table. I decided I would try to talk to him after football practice. But that never happened.

A few minutes into practice that evening, we began a scrimmage drill. The coach had the starters running plays against different defensive lineups his scouts had seen our next opponent use the week before. When it was my turn to play a defensive position, the food thief and one of his friends from his lunch table came directly at me and both made contact at the same time. They said nothing, but I got the message. I didn't shower after practice. I went straight home and spent the night trying to decide what to do.

These were the days before television was generally available. Certainly common folks like us didn't have "television sets" in their bedrooms. And, in fact, on most nights the black and white TV set in the living room of our house could only get two fuzzy channels from Nashville and Louisville. So to pass the time, I sometimes would read a book from my dad's bookshelf. A couple of nights earlier, I had found on dad's chair a book about Will Rogers.

I knew nothing about Will Rogers, but on this night, I was desperate to get my mind off the food thief, because the more I thought about the problem the more confused and afraid I was. Who should I tell about this? What will I say? When should I tell them? Will they even believe me? Will they understand why I waited so long to report this? What will the first-stringers do? What will Coach do? Will it destroy the team? Will I destroy the team? I didn't know the answers, but at least on this night, I knew none of them were good.

I read the book about Rogers until my eyes were so droopy they wouldn't focus. The only passage I remembered when I laid the book down was this bit of advice Rogers had apparently given to any politician who would listen. He told them, "Never miss a good chance to shut up."

I fell asleep with that phrase on my brain, I guess. And when I woke up the morning to deliver my papers, it was almost like Will Rogers was talking to me about the food thief problem. He was saying to me: "Don't tell anyone tomorrow. Wait." I didn't know what might happen later, but by the time I was finished with my route, Will Rogers had convinced me to "shut up" for at least one more day. My decision was to do and to say nothing that day and hope the food thief would not strike again.

It was now Friday. And it did happen again. The same guy walked past me at the cashier's station with a tray full of food and didn't pay for it. This time, he didn't even leave a quarter, and he didn't smile. In the next few minutes, three or four other starters did the same thing, saying nothing, paying nothing and silently daring me to stop them. I did not.

Friday was game night and only those who would dress for the game had to show up at the gym after school. My name, as usual, had not been on the list the day before. I was happy about that, but I knew that now the problem was even worse. After thinking about it the night before, and now adding today's new food thieves to it, I realized that this was probably going to snowball. And sooner or later, somebody would be caught. When that happened, I was sure I would be accused by the school of cooperating with these guys.

Worst of all, the huge fears I had thought about last night still were there; but now they were magnified. If I turned the food thieves in now, would they believe me. Oh crap!! And even if the principal knew I was telling the truth, would he ignore me cause of backlash from football fans? I hadn't even thought about that possibility last night.

And if the principal did believe me, then all the food thieves would be thrown off the team, or at least suspended. That would mean that the much-loved and highly principled Coach would watch his dream season crash. Then the whole town would learn the details and I would be blamed by everybody, especially the school's students and fans, for being the "snitch."

There would be more than one idiot out there who would be stupid enough to become violent. Not a good outcome for anybody, and certainly not for me and my family.

****

A responsible dad who has quiet, thoughtful ways is the greatest gift a teenager can ever experience. I had a dad like that. I made sure I was home early from school and waiting outside when he pulled into our graveled driveway that afternoon. I had never done that before.

I could tell my dad was exhausted after five days on the road, so I just said "Hi, Dad" and walked away. But he knew immediately I needed him. He went into the house, kissed my mom, and as usual, went straight to the refrigerator to get his traditional Friday afternoon beer. Then, instead of going upstairs to change his clothes, he quietly motioned to me to follow him. We went out to the back yard. Mom had no idea what was going on, but she didn't interfere. Dad and I sat at the picnic table we had built together a few months before. I cried with relief as I told him what was happening.

My dad and I attended the football game together that night. I couldn't understand why, but he insisted that I sit in the student section, away from him. He sat in another section of bleachers reserved for Andrew Jackson High School's adult fans, faculty and alums. The principal was two rows behind him.

When halftime came, with Jackson High holding a comfortable lead, I saw my dad talking with the principal. They were standing some distance away from the other fans in the section. They shook hands just as the second half began and went back to their seats. Jackson High continued to dominate on the field and the final score was lopsided. I didn't really care. I just wanted to hear what my dad had to say.

As we walked back to the car after the game, Dad said he had told the principal exactly what I had told him earlier, and that I wanted to tell the truth to the cafeteria manager but I was afraid. He said he thought the principal understood, but he wanted to talk to me privately, without anyone else. The principal would be coming to our house the next morning. Dad said I should tell him everything and not to worry. They had agreed on a way to handle this that they thought would "work out." I didn't know what that meant, but dad said he wanted the principal to explain it to me because it was all his idea. I tossed and turned forever that night and when the alarm clock buzzed at 5 a.m., I turned it off and went back to sleep for almost an hour, so I was really late completing my paper route in the morning.

When I returned to the house, my parents were in the kitchen having coffee. They said I should rest until the principal arrived. Mom knew all about it by then. She said she was sure things would "work out." There were those words again.

My previous contact with the principal was zero. I had seen him drive past me a few times going toward the school when I was on my paper route. That was it. I was nervous when I let him in the front door that morning. My parents greeted him at the door and said they were going to breakfast so we could meet in private.

I thought it would be a pretty long meeting , but it wasn't. The principal said he had gone to his office after last night's game to read my student record. He said it was a good record both for school work and for behavior. Then he asked me to tell him "what happened" and to "name names." He said that he considered this to be an official investigation so I had to tell him everything. He was going to take notes.

I started by telling him about my car and the money I owed my dad. When I finally got to the actual theft and how the guy just dropped a quarter on the counter the first day and nothing on Friday, my voice became real high-pitched. I told him I was really afraid of the guy who took the food on the first day, and because of that I didn't want to use the kid's name. And I told him about Thursday night being alone in my room and the Will Rogers book and hoping nothing would happen on Friday.

He interrupted me to say that I should tell him everything I had told my dad and that he would make certain that nobody from the school would beat me up. He didn't say how he was going to do that, but I guess I believed him because in the next sentence I heard the kid's name come out of my mouth. I told him I was still afraid but I felt better.

After I told him the name of the Thursday Thief, I told him who the Friday thieves were and every detail I could remember. I even told him what most of the food items were on the Thursday Thief's tray that he had not paid for.

When I finished, he closed his note pad and thanked me for telling the truth. He understood why I was afraid to speak to him sooner. He said he had been a big fan of Will Rogers and that I did the right thing by waiting and going to my dad first. He told me there were some things he couldn't tell me or my parents yet because there were more people he had to speak with that day. Then he shocked me. He said he knew the names of all the thieves before he heard them from me. But he had to be sure I wasn't part of the problem. That was the real reason for our meeting.

As he was leaving he told me to be in his office with my dad one hour before classes started on Monday, and that I should not speak to anyone about this until then. By that time he said he would have "everything under control."

Then came the last words he said to me as we walked to his car: "Robert, listen carefully. I know you are afraid of these guys. I have not forgotten what it is like to be afraid. But you have to trust me now. You have done the most important part here. You kept the lid on a very bad situation until adults could get involved. Now it is my job to handle this and I will. No matter what you hear me say on Monday morning, I do not want you or your dad to respond or to show any surprise. I am going to see what I can do today to help Coach make it through the season and still discipline the boys who did this. But no one will know anything about our meeting here today."

I didn't sleep much the next two nights. I kept trying to envision what was going to happen at the meeting on Monday. And I'd bet I repeated to my dad the principal's instruction about remaining silent at least twenty times. Each time, my dad said he understood. He was much more patient with me than usual. Sometime during that weekend, I brought the Will Rogers book out and showed him the page where I had read the words: "Never miss a good chance to shut up." I used that as another chance to remind my dad that was the plan for Monday morning.

There was a large conference room next to the principal's office where the teaching staff and the town school board had meetings. Most of the chairs around the big table were taken by the time my dad and I arrived on Monday morning. The main door to the conference room opened onto the main hallway of the school but that door was locked. The only way in and out was through the principal's private office. No one could enter or even see into the room except those who had been told to attend.

Everybody in the room was quiet. The boys who had stolen the lunch food sat with their heads down, like they were praying. Their parents were all present. So were all of the football coaches and the cafeteria manager, Mrs. Hatch. And seated next to her was Billy Gibson, the other checkout boy who worked with me in the cafeteria. I had totally forgotten about him.

I had no idea if Billy had seen what happened or who he might have told. He looked over at me and shrugged his shoulders as if he was confused. I shrugged my shoulders back at him, as if to say, "Me, too." My dad saw us and immediately made a coughing noise to remind me to remain silent in all ways. At that moment the principal of the school walked in. To my surprise, he was followed by the County Sheriff. They walked to the front and center of the room where a speaker would stand in a public meeting. The principal looked around the room, I guessed he was making one last check to assure every necessary person was present, then he nodded to the Sheriff, who immediately walked back to the entrance door, closed it, and stood in front of it. The message was clear. Nobody was going to leave until this meeting was over. Then the principal began to speak.

I can't quote his words exactly anymore, but this is pretty close: "We are here today because these four boys, who were supposed to be school leaders and heroes, are thieves. Stand up boys so everybody in this room can see who you are. And remain standing while I speak. You have disgraced yourselves, your school and your team. Everyone here should know that these boys have been interviewed by the Sheriff and me in the presence of their parents, and they have admitted stealing food from the school cafeteria. The Sheriff has their signed statements at his office. Mrs. Hatch saw it happen with her own eyes. She saw them on Friday put large amounts of food on their trays and walk right past the student cashiers without paying. And they were laughing about it."

He looked directly at the four standing boys and he said: "All four of you boys should be suspended from school and you should be kicked off the football team. But we have a serious community problem here that the Sheriff, the head coach, the mayor – who is standing back there in the back – and I all recognize. This town has suffered too many bad blows in the last few years. We've had the Mill close down and some other businesses went with it. We've had some racial violence that got us some very bad press.

We have a lot of people out of work. But this year's Jackson High football team has brought a new spirit to the people here that has to be protected. You boys, by your stupid acts of stealing, have created a much bigger problem than you realize. You have put the recovery effort and the little bit of pride we have left in this town in the trash heap. And you left it to us to stick our hands in that dirty trash for the good people of this town and to protect you and your families. If you were suspended from school and the football team was dismantled right now, you four boys might come to serious harm. So, gentlemen, here is the way it's going to be, and you better listen carefully, because there will be no room for any mistake by any one of you.

You are all on strict probation for the rest of the time you are students in this school. One misstep in class, one class failed or dropped, one rule broken, by any one of you, and all of you will be expelled, no questions asked. So you had better study together, attend school together and police one another's behavior.

And speaking of working together, you are all going to be held personally responsible to protect Billy and "Bones," our two cashiers, from any bullying or threats of any kind. Billy didn't see your thefts but "Bones" did. "Bones" did not report your bad conduct because he was afraid of you, and you all knew it. Shame on you for putting your teammate through this. And remember, if there is one incident of bullying against either Billy or "Bones," you will all be expelled.

One more thing. Your confessions and this meeting have been tape recorded. I will keep the tapes. Nobody is to ever know what occurred in this meeting unless I announce it – and I will not hesitate to do that if any one of you guilty boys breaks any rule or smarts off to any teacher or fails to turn in any required homework at any time while you are students here. Believe me, I will take the lid off of this entire matter and you boys and your families will bear the consequences.

Until and unless that happens, you boys and everybody in this room remember this rule when this meeting is over. It comes from a famous American guy named Will Rogers who died in 1935. Will Rogers said: "Never pass up a good chance to shut up."

The Last Season

Evansville Courier & Press
Sunday, August 25, 2002

S O NOW IT BEGINS. The high school soccer season that I've anticipated and dreaded for so long. The last season I will have a child on the field.

The rites of passage that occur as my children grow to adulthood have always been difficult for me. I've watched my older kids pass through this door already. It doesn't get any easier. I would prefer, if I could, to keep them forever in that part of childhood just before the reality of this world's burdens overtakes them. But life doesn't offer that option. Tempus Fugit.

This team that my boy plays with is a special group. They have, most of them, played this game together almost since they learned to walk. They have won together, suffered heartbreaking losses together, and nurtured one another through injuries, surgeries and worse. They hang out together; and they have hung together. They would never admit it, but they love one another.

There is, likewise, a unique relationship among the parents of these boys. Our families are as diverse as can be imagined – economically, socially and in approaches to parenting. But we have traveled the country together; we have raised our glasses together; and we have sent our kids off to distant cities in the care of one another. In that process, we've become an extended family. Every one of these kids is, in a sense, our own. It is a phenomenon that happens over and over in the new world of youth athletics. And that's good. It might be the modern equivalent of the old close-knit neighborhood.

I've known many parents of teenage boys through the years. It's been a fairly common theme among them that the day their boys moved on could not arrive soon enough. I feel precisely the opposite. And so, I believe, do the parents of the other boys in this group of high school seniors.

As this last season begins, the hopes and dreams and goals of these boys are very high. The hopes and dreams and goals their parents hold for them are even higher, but with a slightly different focus. Sure, we'd like to see them win the state championship. And well they might. But we know, even if they don't, they have learned much more on the soccer fields and in the company of one another than how to play a game.

The highest objectives of all those years of training, practices and competition are already in the bag. And those other things they've learned will sustain them when the games are forever over. Loyalty. Dedication to a purpose. Self-discipline. Playing within the rules. Toughness when things go wrong. Graciousness in victory and dignity in defeat. Caring about a brother. How to be a friend. Understanding tough love. The value of hard work. The importance of family and relationships.

When all the games and all the good times traveling to distant fields of competition are only memories, and when we parents have raised our glasses together for the last time, our boys will carry away all of those life skills into a world where we cannot protect them any longer. Those essential lessons from the athletic fields make all the weekends on the road and all the trips to the practice fields worthwhile, no matter whether this team in this season wins or loses.

It'll be great if they manage to hang up a state championship. But the fact is, they are, all of them, already champions. The same is true for the countless other kids on other teams, and in other sports, who work as hard as they can to bring their best efforts to the games they play. They are all champions. They are the purpose and the product of youth sports.

Some years ago, I gave my son a framed gift that hangs on his wall yet today. It is a calligraphy reproduction of a sporting goods ad from long ago. I wish I had written it myself, but I can only take credit for preserving it. Here is what it says:

> Do you want to be an athlete? Because if you do, then you have to remember everyday what it means to always want to be better, to want to be the best. And if you do, then you have to understand that it's not enough just to want to be the best.
>
> You can't just sit around and talk about how much you want it or what you'll do in the

next game. You have to show how much you want it every day. So don't just hope for it. Don't just think about it. Go out and get it. Dare yourself to do everything it takes to be the very best that you can be. And then, whether you win or lose, at worst you'll know exactly who you are, and that you gave it all you had to give. At best, you will know that you are a champion.

My boy and his friends have read those words from time to time. They carry that resolve with them now, as their days together wind down. Indeed, they will carry it with them always. But for now, for the next couple of months, they will still be a group of high school soccer players, united in purpose one last time. So, let the games begin. Godspeed, boys, and good luck. Tempus Fugit.

Summertime

Evansville Courier & Press
Friday, March 3, 2000

SOMETIMES I THINK about summer in the middle of the winter. When I do, I remember when I was very young and baseball was at the center of my summer times. I played baseball, read about baseball and lived baseball; and anyone who didn't was no friend of mine.

All I really knew about the "big" league players I read on baseball cards and in the newspaper box scores. I had thousands of baseball cards. They were 5¢ a pack with a big flat piece of bubble gum included. I bought 'em with money from my paper route. The last time I saw those baseball cards, they were in my closet, neatly divided by team and year. It was just before we moved. My mother was very efficient. She did not keep "junk." That's why I am still working for a living.

In those days, the big leagues were no more real to me than flying saucers. The closest big league team was a five hour drive away. Mickey, Willie and the Duke were names in newspaper reports and snippets in newsreels at the Woodlawn Theater. Nothing more. The real professional baseball teams in my life were the Evansville Braves and their rivals from Terre Haute, Quincy,

Springfield, Cedar Rapids, Burlington and the rest of the Three I League. Three I – you know, Illinois, Iowa and Indiana.

In 1953, when I was 10, Bosse Field was six blocks from my house. Six blocks from home was walking distance in those days – even for a ten year old at night. Bosse Field is where, every summer, the Evansville Braves played their home games. Horace Garner was their right fielder. Horace was a big, strong black guy who could hit a baseball really hard. One night, he hit one that flew over the right field brick wall, bounced on the pavement of Heidelbach Avenue and broke a window in the Hoosier Cardinal plastics factory across the street. Mark and Sammy could probably do that today, but not very often.

Paul Cave was one of my heroes too. He was a pitcher for the Braves. The best one they ever had if you ask me.

Horace and Paul were my friends. We were on a first- name basis, and I was welcome in their homes. At least they'd let me in when I showed up at their doors. The way I got to know them was because I sold ice cream bars at Bosse Field every summer night the Braves were in town from 1953 to 1956. I always got there early and stayed late so I could hang around the players and talk about baseball during practice and after the games. Horace and Paul were good people; and they were patient with a kid who thought they were gods.

I earned a penny for every ice cream bar I sold. That usually meant I'd make about a buck a night. Big money for a pre-teen in the 1950s. But when Paul pitched, I didn't sell much ice cream. I never strayed more than 4 rows in either direction from dead behind home plate when he was on the mound. I still think he had the best curve ball I've ever seen. I was also temporarily out of business every time Horace came to bat. As far as I was concerned, Horace was the equal of Mickey, Willie and the Duke. Except he was real and I could watch him play and I could talk to him almost anytime I wanted to. Forget the money. My real pay was that I got into the ball park for free and the players were my friends.

What a great deal that was for a 10 year old! The only better job would have been to be the Braves' bat boy. Just imagine! A Braves uniform. Sitting in the dugout right next to those guys. All the cracked bats you could ever want. And I think the pay was at least $2 a night. But to be a bat boy for the Evansville Braves required connections. I didn't even know what "connections" were. But I knew I wanted to get into the ball park when the Braves were in town. And I knew I didn't have the 25 cents to buy a ticket every night. And I knew they hired kids to sell stuff there.

So one Spring day when I was riding my bike around the neighborhood, I saw the gate to Bosse Field open. I rode right through the gate and almost ran right into this old guy walking down the ramp. I stopped and asked this old guy if I could get a job selling ice cream or peanuts at the ball games because I loved the Braves, but I couldn't pay to get in every night. I talked real fast so I could tell him everything before he threw me out. The old guy turned out to be Bob Coleman. He was the Braves' manager; and I would have recognized him in a baseball uniform. But he looked a lot different in street clothes, so I didn't know who he was.

If there is a heaven, Bob Coleman is there right now. He loved baseball and young people and he was good to both. If that won't get you into heaven, I don't want to go there. Bob Coleman took me straight to a guy named Eddie and, right there on the spot, Eddie hired me to sell ice cream bars at the games, and that's how I met Horace and Paul.

I started work that same night; and I sold ice cream at every Evansville Braves home game during the next four summers of my life. I wish I still had that job. It was the best one I've ever had. I was part of the ball game, part of the team. I felt good when I was there. In fact, I've never felt better.

A Christmas Lesson

THE ORIGINAL SANDLEBEN'S drug store was at the corner of Harriet and Oregon Streets. That is where, during the holiday season of 1953, a most exciting contest was held. I lived only four houses away in the same block on Harriet Street.

This was a neighborhood where everybody knew everybody else. Any boy who went astray was soon reported to his parents for appropriate discipline.

In late November there appeared in the huge front window of Sandleben's a magnificent red bicycle. This bike would be the prize to the winner of the contest. Next to the bike was the second prize, an electric train set, and next to that, the third prize, a new 45 rpm record player.

The contest was open only to children who would not yet be twelve on Christmas day. It would begin the morning after Thanksgiving Day and continue until noon on Christmas Eve. When a customer made a purchase at Sandleben's, every penny the customer spent would count as one vote for any child the customer designated. The child with the most votes at noon on Christmas Eve would win the bike.

I wanted that red bicycle really bad. But so did several other neighborhood kids, especially a boy named Tommy, who lived a few blocks away on Mary Street. Tommy was eleven. I was ten. He was always pretty nice to me, but the only times we really played together were in the sandlot baseball and alley basketball games that never seem to happen anymore. So I didn't know him well.

I knew that Tommy lived with his mom in the back half of a small shotgun house. He wasn't a trouble-maker, but he ran the streets pretty much whenever and wherever he wanted because his mom wasn't home very much. He didn't have a dad in his house. He didn't have a bike either.

My bike was an old hand-me-down from one of my cousins. It was pretty rickety, but whenever it broke my dad could always fix it. My dad didn't make a lot of money, but he had a steady job and he could fix anything. And even though my dad traveled a lot, he was always there when I needed him. Not so for Tommy. His dad was never there.

When the contest started on the day after Thanksgiving, Tommy and I and bunch of other kids were on the sidewalk just outside the main door into Sandleben's. Every time a customer approached, it was bedlam. Every kid screamed his own name and asked for the customer's vote. Most of the customers didn't know about the contest. And because of all the shouting, they didn't have a clue what all the excitement was about. Some of them would stop and ask, but then every kid would answer at the same time, and nothing good would come of it.

After an hour or so of that chaos, I walked home, frustrated and dejected. I walked through the back door and slumped into a chair at the kitchen table. I had lost all hope of winning the contest.

But a few minutes later my dad came home. My brooding silence was not lost on him. He sat down and asked what was wrong. I explained the contest to him and the wild scene at the corner. The conversation that followed was the beginning of some lessons well-learned.

Dad said yelling at customers coming to the drug store was not the way to win the contest. He was sure the Sandleben family would not let that continue anyway. He told me I should go down there to meet customers only when there was not a crowd of other kids around. And then, I should speak quietly and politely. He told me to make little cards with my name on them to give to the customers. He said I should go around the neighborhood and around my paper route and talk to the people I knew. And he said I should call my aunts and uncles and ask them to go to Sandleben's whenever they needed something, and to vote for me.

Then Dad gave me a dime and sent me to Sandleben's to buy some index cards. He told me to cut each card into three pieces and to write my name on each piece. He said it was going to be a long contest, and soon many of the kids would get tired of chasing customers at the corner and quit. So he told me to be patient, and to knock on neighbor's doors while the other kids were standing on the corner. He said there would be quiet times to hand out my cards at the corner, and politely ask for votes.

I followed my dad's advice. I made my name cards and started knocking on doors. And, sure enough, over the next few days, the crowd of kids on the corner dwindled quickly, just like dad said.

But Tommy was almost always there. He was nice to me when we were working the corner together, but he did his best to get to the approaching customers first. I had already talked to many of them at their houses, so I just gave them my name card.

I learned during conversations with Tommy that, in addition to having a dad and an old bike, I had one more advantage. Tommy didn't have any other family in town. I had lots of relatives who were regular customers at Sandleben's. In fact, my mom had grown up with four brothers and four sisters in the house where we lived. And my Aunt Jo and her husband, Charlie, lived right across the street from Sandleben's.

I stuck to dad's plan. I worked the neighborhood, especially my paper route, spent time at the corner when it wasn't crawling with other kids, and reminded all my aunts and uncles to shop at Sandleben's.

Since Tommy didn't have any relatives or a paper route, and no campaign advisor like my dad, his only plan was to ask for votes at Sandleben's corner whenever he could. And that is what he did. Except for school hours, he didn't miss a minute on that corner.

Every Saturday, I had to collect from my paper route customers and ride my bike downtown to pay my bill. So until late afternoon, Tommy had the corner pretty much to himself. During the week, if my homework was finished, I could stay on the corner until eight o'clock. Nobody checked Tommy's homework, and he didn't have a curfew. So he could stay every night until Sandleben's closed at ten.

On Sundays, when the drug store was closed, I canvassed the neighborhood for votes. I remember getting amused looks from many of the adults who heard my little speech about the contest and how much I wanted that red bike. They were mostly people who knew my mom and dad well. And they probably knew that if I really needed a bike, my parents could find a way to get one for me. But they listened, and smiled, and took my name card.

The contest standings were posted in the drug store window each Saturday. From the first week to the last, Tommy and I were neck and neck, with one of us in the lead. Some weeks he would pull ahead a little bit; other weeks it would be me. We managed to stay friendly, but we were both working hard to win. On the last Saturday before Christmas Eve, I was about 300 votes ahead. That meant that only three dollars of votes separated us.

In those final days, I called all of my aunts and uncles again and spent as much time as I could down on the corner greeting customers and handing out name cards. Tommy was there too, and by this time, he had made his own name cards. They were neater than mine. I didn't know what else he was doing to get votes, but I knew he wouldn't give up.

On the morning of Christmas Eve, Tommy and I were both at the corner before the drug store opened. It was a busy morning and we both did our best to hustle votes. I felt like Tommy was doing a little better than me that morning.

Then, at about 11:30, just before the contest deadline, my Uncle Charlie came from his house, walking to the drug store. At almost the same time, my dad walked toward us from my house. They greeted Tommy and me just like any other customers would, and walked into Sandleben's together. I could tell that Tommy was pretty worried. I'm sure he thought what I thought—my Uncle would buy a carton of cigarettes, and my dad would spend a little money, and they would put me over the top. But Tommy didn't say a word to me. He just continued greeting customers and handing out his cards.

My dad and Uncle Charlie were in the store for quite a while. They came out together just before noon, each with a sack and a smile. Uncle Charlie crossed the street and went into his house. My dad told me it was time for lunch and asked Tommy if he would like to join us.

Tommy said no; he wanted to wait for the final votes to be counted. I didn't ask my dad what was in his sack.

Mom had a big meal ready. Santa always arrived early on Christmas Eve at our house, so she knew this was the last meal her children would have until the presents were opened that night. I couldn't eat. All I could think about was that red bike that would soon be mine. I was sure of it because of the recent smiles from my dad and uncle.

But just as we finished our meal, there came a loud knock on our back door. It was Tommy. He was shouting "I won, I won, I won the bike." My dad congratulated Tommy, as I looked at them in disbelief. I jumped up and ran down to the corner to see the final standings in the drug store window. Tommy was right. He had won by about a hundred points and I had finished second.

When I got back home, Tommy was using our telephone to call his mom at work to tell her the news. He was so happy he could hardly speak. My dad said I should congratulate Tommy, so I did—but they both knew I didn't mean it. This was going to be the worst Christmas of my life.

I went upstairs to my room to sulk. My dad didn't follow me. No one did. A while later, as the sun was setting, I looked out my window at the street just as Tommy rode past on his new red bike. I was not happy.

It was a tradition in my family that a few days before Christmas, the front room of our house, where the

Christmas tree stood, would be blocked from view so Santa could do his work whenever he chose. A large blanket was tacked up from floor to door-top so that no little eyes could see what was going on in there. There was a fireplace in that room, Santa's access of course. There was also a never-used door from the front porch, because our old Victorian house had another front door into a foyer. I never thought of that extra door as a door at all. But I guess Santa's helpers did.

Another tradition was that at exactly six o'clock on every Christmas Eve, my dad's parents would arrive for a Christmas celebration that would end just in time for us all to go to Midnight Mass. After a spiked eggnog or two, the blanket would come down and the Christmas bounty would flow.

I wasn't in the Christmas spirit when my grandparents arrived, but my dad was in rare form, telling them about the Sandleben's contest, and how proud he was that I had finished second. I didn't respond with the smile he wanted, but I knew better than to protest. My dad could be a stern disciplinarian, even on Christmas Eve.

Soon it was time for the big event. The Christmas music was playing from our new Victrola and my three younger siblings were in Christmas heaven as the blanket came down and the front room came to life with a huge decorated tree and piles of presents around it. I took a seat quietly in the corner. There were gifts being passed to everyone, and several came my way. But I was too hung up on that red bike to act happy.

When all the gifts had been passed out, my dad took me into the kitchen. We were alone. He closed the door so no one else could hear. He told me he was proud of my work during the contest, but he was very disappointed in my behavior since Tommy won the bike. He never raised his voice, but he told me I was selfish and ungrateful.

"You are a lucky little boy, David", he said to me. "You worked hard to win, but Tommy worked hard, too. If Tommy had not won the Sandleben's bike, he probably never would have a bike at all, much less a new one. Tommy's dad died in the war and he has so little. His mom works two jobs. He has no one at home to help him and still, he's a pretty good kid. He deserves that bike. I want you to think about that, David." That was all my dad said. Then he returned to the happiness that filled the front room.

I went to my room and did what he said—I thought about it. Mostly, I thought about those few words that struck me hardest: "Tommy's dad died in the war and he has so little."

When we went to midnight mass that night, I thanked the Baby Jesus for my mom and my dad and even for my brothers and sister. And I thanked Him for my house and for my grandparents, too. And I thanked him for letting Tommy win. I told him my old bike was okay. Then I went home and to sleep.

When morning came, I stumbled down the stairs and into the kitchen. Breakfast was on the stove and my dad and Uncle Charlie were having coffee at the table.

Mom kissed me good morning and my little sister told me "Merry Christmas."

I said, "Yep, Dad, you were right last night. I am pretty lucky. I'm glad Tommy won. And we'll have fun with that electric train, won't we?"

My dad and Uncle Charlie smiled. They said they had something to tell me. They said they had both voted for Tommy yesterday. At that moment, I understood everything my dad had told me, and I felt even better. I felt like Christmas.

Then, my dad said there was one more present by the tree for me. He said I could go get it and bring it into the kitchen.

The soft glow from the Christmas Tree lights was all that lit the living room as I walked in. And there, in front of the tree, with a big silver bow on it, stood a beautiful red bike. Just like Tommy's.

The House at 923 State Street

AT THE INTERSECTION of Jones and State Streets in St. Joseph, Michigan, there stands an old Victorian relic. Officially, it is 923 State Street. To me, however, that is not an address. It is the name of the Old Victorian Lady that came back from near oblivion to become a well-spring of family, excitement and memories.

When first we met, I resented and mistrusted her. After some time passed, I resigned myself to her involvement in my life. Eventually I came to cherish her central role as the family sanctuary, the vessel of its history, and the welcoming hostess of lives well-lived. She witnessed the birth of relationships, the cultivation of friendships, and the homecomings. She saw the tragedies, reunions, impromptu banquets and planned celebrations. She welcomed all new arrivals at the front door, whether or not they were expected. Rare was the evening when she was not lit up like party-central for more than 50 years. And on her watch, I did some serious growing up in a very short period of time.

In service to my family, 923 State Street revealed a heart, soul and warmth that fed the spirits of her occupants and conveyed an energy of noisy serenity to all who crossed her threshold. She smiles. She makes her family and guests feel better. Her creaks and groans speak to them, and of them. She is the tabernacle of a family and, in my case, the keeper of the grail from which I poured the last drops of childhood and drank important sips of maturity.

Dad

The Great Depression interrupted my Dad's education when he completed high school in 1934. Despite his numerous talents, creativity and desire to excel, there was simply no money available for him to pay for college. Consequently, he went straight from high school to the factory floor. He attended trade school at night and. at age 20, he became the youngest precision tool and die maker in the city. He had unique mechanical and interpersonal talents, too. It did not take long for the brass at Servel to recognize those attributes.

During World War II, Dad made the tooling and dies for the most intricate parts of the fighter aircraft used by the U.S. in the war effort. When the war ended, he was quickly taken off the factory floor to become Servel's "last-resort" national service representative. In that job, he was dispatched to repair defective refrigerators and other malfunctioning Servel appliance products that nobody else could repair. In 1956, he was hired to fill a similar position with Whirlpool, another appliance manufacturer. By 1960, when he was 43, he was competing for advancement against many younger college graduates for whom the "G.I. Bill" had paid college expenses.

■■

Dad's Promotion

In early July of 1960, Dad was "offered" a promotion. If he accepted the offer, he would have to relocate to St. Joseph, Michigan, from southwestern Indiana. It was one of those offers "you can't refuse." This promotion was critical to his career. He had been chosen over all those college grads that he had been matched against for so many years.

I fully understood Dad's decision to take the new position. If he declined, there would be no more opportunities, no more offers for advancement. And, in fact, his new job required him to start an entirely new department to train the service representatives from all over the country. If he didn't run that new department, he would probably then have to work under the person who did take the job, and we would be moving to Michigan anyway.

My self-centered 17-year-old self didn't like that at all, and I was not happy. I had lived my entire life in one city. My senior year in high school, all my friends, including a long-time girlfriend, all of my identity and all of my roots were about to be taken away, and I had zero control. But I had to confront reality. My family was going to move to Michigan and there was nothing I could do about it.

I was the oldest of four children and very close to my dad. He had to start working in his new position on August 1st. He would have to leave his wife and family in Southern Indiana until he could find a suitable house, which was going to be difficult in St. Joseph. Dad would be living in a motel for "a while."

Hello St. Joe

After some long and difficult discussions, my parents and I agreed that I should not change high schools in the middle of my senior year. I would go with Dad to St. Joe and enroll in the small Catholic high school there. So late in July, Dad and I became weekday residents of Room 106 at the Golden Link Motel, 360 miles from our roots. We arrived on a Saturday, two days before the football team's practices began.

Until school classes commenced, I went to football practice each morning and then hung with the new friends I met among the football players. They treated me well. By the day classes began, I had met all 37 of my senior classmates . . . that's right – 37. I found my ego boosted because I was suddenly the fastest runner on my football team instead of just being one of the average speed ball carriers. And on pass plays, my new friend, Bob Jochem, and I were the two principal targets of our quarterback.

Both Bob and I were tall and easy to spot. Bob was also a genuine and fearless three-sport athlete. He soon became my closest friend. The rest of the team was pretty good, too. We finished the season with 8 wins and 1 loss – good enough for a share of the league championship. Instead of being just another face in the crowd, I was the new kid from Indiana who helped put the 1960 St. Joseph Ponies football team over the top.

Difficult Times

As time passed, however, the stress of motel living, the long every-weekend travel back and forth between St. Joseph and southern Indiana, and the sadness of being separated permanently from my old coaches, friends and teachers, wore me down. By the end of October, the steady chill winds from the lake began to blow, loneliness and depression took me over, and my behavior both in school and with my Dad was often disrespectful and impatient. I don't know how or why, but Dad and the nuns remained patient with me. So were my classmates and teammates.

No matter how hard I tried, I couldn't shake my anger and depression. The die was cast. Transferring from a school with a senior class of 250 to one with a class of 38, including me, was a social shock that I did not always handle with grace. I am now grateful to that small class at St. Joe Catholic High School and the nuns who taught there for their patience. Because of the kindness with which they all treated me, I now make special efforts to attend every reunion event held by the members of that senior class. By November, 1960, I was awash in self-pity and not a pleasant person to be around. The long Michigan winter was just beginning, "lake-effect" snow fell daily, the wind off the lake was biting cold and relentless; and literally nothing could make me happy. I was certain things could not get any worse. My life was already upside down. But from my point of view, things did get worse.

■■■

The House

Dad's search for a house in St. Joe where his family could live also stretched into November. Again, my self-centered self didn't take into account that he, too, was under considerable pressure. More so than I was, I now realize. The primary source of his pressure was his wife, my mother, who had been a "single mom" of three for more than three months. And she didn't like it one little bit. She had more or less "demanded" (if you know what I mean) that Dad find housing for the family in St. Joe. There were very few houses available for sale, and most that were couldn't accommodate a family of six. I was only vaguely aware of his increasing desperation, but I did notice that I was alone in the motel room while he was out house hunting every afternoon before dinner.

To my great dismay, he told me one evening in early November that he was seriously considering the purchase of 923 State Street. I couldn't imagine a worse choice. He had driven me past every private residence that was for sale in or near St. Joe, including that one. From the street, the house at 923 State Street looked to me like it was going to fall down any minute. I thought a wrecking ball would bring it merciful rest. It had to be almost 100 years old, and, I thought, haunted. But availability, size and price were foremost in my dad's mind, and due to its age and appearance, 923 State Street was empty, cheap and had five bedrooms. Desperate people do desperate things. When he asked me to go with him to inspect "that old house on State Street," I agreed but felt an immediate wave of nausea.

In what now seems the blink of an eye, fifty-five years and more have passed since that day I first stepped onto the grounds of 923 State Street. Up close, she was a pitiful sight – a battered, bruised and shabby old lady. Nothing of her dignity and character was apparent to me in that moment. Mine, though, were the eyes and mind-set of a seventeen-year-old boy whose life was adrift. I saw no hint of any potential in that house to replace the home we had left in Indiana. What I did not and could not know then was that both I and the Old Victorian Lady were about to undergo major transformations. And the same person was going to be responsible for both.

When we entered 923 State Street that day, it was immediately obvious she was well past the onset of decline. The ancient hardwood oak floors were a filthy black and they squeaked, groaned and crackled in protest to the weight of every footstep. The main stairway to the second floor rose from the old-time entrance foyer just inside the front door. Every riser, from bottom to top, screamed its objection. I remember telling dad that these floors would defeat a cat burglar every time.

In both sound and appearance, the house and its stairway were perfect for the set of an Alfred Hitchcock movie. In fact, the entire place looked very much like Hitchcock and his film crew had just departed. Every room was filled with musty-smelling furniture left there when the elderly lady who had owned it was carried out to the hearse several months before.

I could feel the ghost of the recently deceased owner at my hip as I walked from room to dusty room. The power was off. It was dark and cold. There were 19th century steam heat radiators and fire-prone push button light switches in every room. It was a time warp. Creepy. The November wind whistled its way through the cracked window frames. I was spooked.

Dad said little as we moved about, but his inspection was serious and thorough. He was not concerned about ghosts. He was concerned about the structure, and I knew that he liked what he saw. At dinner after the inspection, my worst fears were confirmed. He was upbeat. "That house has real possibilities," he said as he sipped his martini. And in that moment, in the Chicken Nook Café – all the fried chicken and mashed potatoes I could eat for $3.75 – I knew I was destined to live at 923 State Street. I was only partially joking when I told him I might run away, but I knew I wouldn't abandon him. We were in this together and, anyway, the ghost at my hip had passed up every opportunity to bother me. I have since come to regard her as a docent who wanted to change my mind.

••

Transformation

Two weeks later, after numerous promises by dad that he would remodel and restore 923 State Street, install a completely new and modern kitchen and make it a place she would be proud to own, Mom made a tearful visit to St Joseph, walked quickly through the house, cried yet again, signed the papers and drove back to Indiana.

The boy that I was on that day was certain Dad had promised more than he could deliver. As soon as Mom drove away, I told him I would try to help him do this impossible job. He smiled and thanked me, but he knew my skill level and experience in such matters was absolute zero. The smile on his face was one of pure confidence. It was a "game on" smile. The project commenced immediately – that night, in fact. I helped mostly by staying well out of the way and watching my determined and resourceful dad call upon the quiet inner strength born of his Great Depression youth. He worked deep into every night and weekend, turning the old girl's interior into a Victorian showplace. The outside would have to await kinder weather. Walls and ceilings were re-plastered and painted, wood trim and hardwood floors were cleaned, sanded and refinished. They shined as if new. All of the electric wiring and light fixtures were replaced and the most advanced kitchen appliances were installed. And every wall and ceiling were given three coats of fresh paint. I was present during most of the work but of little help. I could paint a wall, lift heavy objects, steady a ladder, fetch a tool and sweep a floor. Otherwise, I was basically useless.

Meanwhile, however, the boy in me was undergoing major and permanent changes as well. Watching my dad toil night after night, I could only marvel at how tireless he was. He was driven by an inner strength I had never seen before in anybody. He had accepted this monumental challenge all alone, and he was meeting it head-on, without complaint or self-pity. He worked for his employer all day and for his family all night. I will never forget what I watched him achieve during those three months.

By the end of March, 1961, the interior of the Old Victorian Lady was transformed and ready for our family. She still creaked and groaned and flexed under the weight of her occupants, and she still needed an exterior facelift that would take place in the summertime, but there was an unmistakable energy of pride, warmth and strength throughout her rooms. And at night, the lights streaming from her twinkled off the melting Spring snow. She was airtight and ready for the onslaught of a family full of life and the frequent gales crossing the Lake Michigan shoreline only 3 blocks away.

So, in the early springtime, through unfamiliar doorways and into her embrace, came a family with uncertain bearings but relieved to be reunited, and 923 State Street emerged from her dark past, rejuvenated, noisy and full of activity. From that moment, there were always the sounds and the energy of the family and of visiting relatives and friends of every generation. Never has a large front porch been more inviting and useful on summer days and evenings. Never has a front door opened and closed so often. And most surely, never had 923 State Street hosted so many visitors from other places. And she did so while providing the perfect environment for a family of lives amid the usual daily surprises, struggles, stumbles, adventures and triumphs, large and small.

Memories were made weekly, especially in the summertime, with countless relatives and friends from near and far arriving and departing in constant succession. The guestrooms were almost always occupied, relationships were preserved and celebrated. Sand from the nearby beaches was everywhere, tracked in by aunts, uncles, cousins, friends of cousins and friends, all visiting and all welcome. Impromptu visitors around cocktail time and twelve or more at the dinner table were common. Every family should be so fortunate.

I had no notion until many years later that I had subconsciously anointed her as hallowed ground. Instead, I regarded 923 State Street as a monument to my dad's inner strength. However, as time passed, I came to understand that, because of his example, it was during those months that I began to appreciate the burdens of personal responsibility that come with being a husband and a father.

Many years later, after Mom had passed away, I was visiting Dad on a weekend of the final summer he would occupy 923 State Street. He was 90 years old and his mind was as sharp as it was at age 20. It was a cool summer evening, so we sat in the parlor with soft music coming from one of the programmed music channels. I heard the Old Victorian Lady creak and groan involuntarily several times. I asked him if those noises bothered him when he was alone there. He said: "None of the sounds this house makes ever bothers me. She is an old soul, just like me, and she speaks her mind. She has made those noises ever since the first time we came in here."

With that remark, I was reminded of those early days we spent in the Golden Link Motel, Room 106, and how tirelessly he had worked to bring this Old Victorian Lady back to life, including the room we were sitting in. And, for perhaps the first time, I told him how much I had admired the dedication that he had shown during that massive reconditioning project and how he had affected me be that example.

Dad's reaction was one of modest surprise. He said, "I just did what was necessary at the time." He said that in those days he had considered himself fortunate, both in his job promotion and in his love for his family, and he simply did what was required to justify and preserve both of them. "It was a hard time for your mother. I had to get her up here, and this was the only place I could find. There wasn't any other option. And it all worked out fine, didn't it?"

I was surprised by his powerful simplicity. In it he expressed a different life lesson than I had taken from his purchase and single-handed renovation of 923 State Street. I told him I had never even considered the linkage between his job promotion achievement and his dedication to wife and family that compelled the rejuvenation of 923 State Street.

Dad's response was immediate. Not only were the job promotion and the remediation linked, they were the "Yin" and the "Yang" of the same love that motivated him every day. He pursued a better job so that his family, especially his wife, could have a better life. And he bought and fixed up 923 State Street for the same reason – because he loved his wife.

I told him that I now had learned two important things as a result of watching him transform 923 State Street: I learned then that every young man should have, as I did, a required "I GET IT" moment in the journey from childhood to responsible manhood – a moment when he comprehends that, in the world of grownups, respect and achievement are earned, not given. Then, on this night, I had learned in this conversation, about 50 years later, what was the very foundation of my Dad's belief system: "WHEN YOU LOVE SOMEBODY, THERE IS NO OPTION. YOU DO WHAT IS NECESSARY."

Dad said nothing in reply. I said nothing more to him, but I did say something to myself. I said: "No wonder everybody admires this man so much."

We continued our quiet evening together in the parlor of the Old Victorian Lady at 923 State Street. And the Lady continued to "speak her mind."

Image by artist Thomas J. Singel
(the author's deceased cousin)

Male Basher

CAUTION: READERS ARE ADVISED IN ADVANCE THAT THE FOLLOWING COMMENTARY CONTAINS MATERIAL THAT MAY BE OFFENSIVE TO SOME INDIVIDUALS WHO ARE OVER-THE-TOP FEMINISTS AND ALSO MAY BE BEYOND THE COMPREHENSION OF MEN AND WOMEN WHO ARE LOST-CAUSE GENDER CHAUVANIST PIGS OF EITHER SEX

THE BUMPER STICKER on the van in front of me said, "All men are idiots and I married their king." The poison of the "Gender War" days continues to infect some small minds here and there, including the lady who was driving that van.

I wondered immediately whether the lady had any notion what that bumper sticker said about her. She had, after all, apparently chosen to marry the "King Idiot." Nobody made her do it. In addition, it appeared from my further observation that she had also voluntarily engaged in activities with the King Idiot which resulted in the presence of the young child who occupied the infant safety seat just behind her. Assuming that was the case, I then wondered why she would want to procreate with any idiot, much less the king of all idiots. But, I couldn't ask her those questions, so I just hoped the baby in the backseat was a kick-ass boy, and I made a wish that God would bless her with ten more babies, all boys, and each the reincarnation of Genghis Kahn.

I was relieved when the van turned from my route. I had no desire to spend my energy fuming at some female idiot who had gone to the expense to purchase a sign to publicly complain that she had married the king of all the idiots, and then put that sign in a place where everybody could see that she had compounded the problem by having sex with his highness.

In fairness, a couple decades ago, when the Gender War was raging, there were some serious issues of educational, social and employment fairness to women that required attention. That has largely happened. But the very fact that there was a Gender War was evidence that men and women are fundamentally different in many good respects. And part of the legacy of that war is the notion that those fundamental differences, taken together, are facts to be celebrated and appreciated. They make life interesting for everybody and have a lot to do with the continuation of the human race. Those differences should not be the bases for hateful, hurtful, demeaning or denigrating remarks.

Nevertheless, fifteen years and more into the 21st Century, a day rarely passes when I don't hear someone making such remarks. And it is almost always a woman, in conversation with – yes – another woman, bashing her husband, her male partner, boyfriend, male co-worker, men in general, or all of the above. Moreover, the bashing is usually supplemented by the disclosure of the basher's version of a very private matter that should never leave a couple's bedroom.

It's a strange paradox. Women, it seems, are free openly to demean at will any male or group of males that currently irritates their tender sensibilities; while most males, especially in the workplace, pursue "politically correct" language and behavior around their female co-workers as if their jobs depend upon it. And, in fact, their jobs do depend on it. So they converse as though they are in church, afraid that some inadvertent remark or harmless glance at a "liberated" woman will cost them their jobs and their families and land them in court.

I willingly concede that men in general, and most especially guys in the 18 to 40-year-old age range, often are inconsiderate, stupid and immature. Guys surrender their childhoods grudgingly – some never do. If you require proof of that, just tune your TV to America's Funniest Videos some evening and watch a thirty-year-old father and husband do something really stupid like riding a bicycle off the roof of a two-story house on a dare. It is not true of all men, but a fair percentage of them have no internal governor of their behavior when they are at play, and yet another percentage is genetically prone to allowing his interior governor to take a day off every once in a while. But every woman knows those things about men. That doesn't make such stupid behavior okay or excusable, but it is the nature of the beast.

The type of attitude exemplified by the lady with the King Idiot bumper sticker is a perfect example of the consequences. What a woman can easily observe in a man's demeanor, habits and perceptions of romance during courtship is precisely what she can expect if she marries the dude. Guys, in the main, have neither the guile nor the stamina to behave in a manner inconsistent with their real selves for any sustained period.

So, if a guy repeatedly does stupid stuff or makes stupid remarks, or if he plays golf a lot, or doesn't always listen carefully to what his girlfriend says, or if he forgets her birthday before the wedding, that is probably what will happen after the wedding. If, during courtship, a man flirts with other women or is unfaithful to his girlfriend or doesn't always tell the truth – guess what? The girlfriend should probably look elsewhere, because that guy's stripes will not change when he puts on a wedding ring.

Unfortunately, the same is not true in reverse. What a male person sees and feels and hears from his lady during courtship is frequently precisely the opposite of what he will see, feel and hear when the courtship ends and the marriage begins. And at the top of that list is s-e-x.

The most alluring and attractive traits that women display in abundance during courtship, such as smiles, libidos and patience, very often simply go into cold storage after the wedding and, in many cases, that is where they stay. These women then immediately replace those attractive qualities with a mile-long list of complaints about their man's personal habits and behavior, all of which they knew about long before. Men, on the other hand, are universally unaffected by the wedding ceremony. It changes them not at all. It is no surprise, then, to find that men are shocked to discover how much a marriage changes their new wives.

If a man was an irresponsible boy, so he will be as a man, married or not. If he was a responsible boy, he'll be a responsible adult.

And, no matter his responsibility quotient, his age, his marital status or whether he is working or playing or resting, he will think a lot about s-e-x. And about how he'd like to be having some. And he will expect his wife to be just as responsive as his girlfriend was.

Apparently, many women forget after the honeymoon to think enough about s-e-x and forget that their husbands are going to want to engage in s-e-x with their wives at least as often as they did with their girlfriends.

And those women who do forget that fact will very likely soon find themselves in divorce court or attending support groups with other women whose husbands have run off with women who DO think about s-e-x; or at least act that way while they are runnin' off with the support group's husbands.

Of course this pattern works in reverse as well. If a new husband fails to continue in the same pattern of attentiveness and romantic engagement and responsible behavior he followed as a boyfriend, he has misrepresented himself and the marriage is doomed, because most women hate – really hate – to be lied to. However, in many of these cases, the divorce is preceded by a prolonged period of miserable cohabitation and often a couple of children who are innocent victims of the mess because women like to think they can "fix" the problem by changing the husband. Trust me on this one – Men do not change. Women change, but men do not change.

So, back to the woman with the male bashing bumper sticker and the ladies we all hear in hateful conversation about their mates. Ladies, be careful when you make your marital choices. It is literally true that what you see is what you get. If you do not approve of the maturity, responsibility level and sexual expectations of a male companion, do not walk away from him – RUN.

As for those women who are inclined to bash males by public signage or in public discussions, don't do it. That kind of behavior says more about your choices and your judgment than it says about your mate. And remember, he is God's product, not yours.

God won't change him and you can't. And if you want a husband but you don't like s-e-x, either make that clear to him during courtship or send him away and go hang out with your girlfriends. You will spare yourself and some poor slob the pain of a miserable marriage.

And guys, if you really love a girl, don't try to fool her by pretending you're someone you're not. You have to be yourself, because you are not clever enough to be anything else. If you just be yourself, you will ether attract her or you won't. It's okay to be male. It's okay to think about s-e-x and to run with your friends. It's okay to care more about baseball than you do about her. Just let her know all these things before you marry her and don't hold anything back. You'll be better off and so will she. And she won't have any excuse for making you the object of her male bashing bumper stickers. If, in the end, she decides you're a stupid slob and you shouldn't get married, you will still be a bachelor. Worse things could happen.

Phyllis Diller was offering a slice of wisdom to both genders when she said that the definition of the term "bachelor" is "a person who doesn't make the same mistake once."

Civility

THIS IS ABOUT EVERY DAY, common civility – or, in my mother's parlance, "manners."

A few evenings ago, I tuned my TV to a political debate. At least that's what the candidates and the media said it was. But it was not a debate. It was a shouting match, complete with rude interruptions, personal attacks, suggestions of dishonesty and fever-pitched voices. These people did not mind their manners. Consequently, we who were watching to help us decide for whom to vote were, instead, required to decide first if we cared to listen to two adults bicker like teenage sisters. I did not. So I watched a ball game instead.

The next day, I was driving in morning traffic on our local excuse for an expressway. The cars and trucks around me were bumper to bumper, with an occasional car length between vehicles. I heard a horn and looked to my right. There was a frantic woman driving the car next to me who was angry at the woman in front of her because that woman had allowed the car in front of her to get two car lengths ahead of her. I shook my head in wonderment.

And then, do you know what the lady in the car next to me did? She gave me the finger. This made me shake my head even more. I mean, I wasn't even the driver she was mad at. Then she did it again, this time screaming obscenities. Pretty crappy way to start the day.

Later that day I was on a conference call with a lawyer from a big city. It did not go well. Ten minutes into the conversation I had to tell the big city lawyer that I did not care to listen to her rude and condescending remarks, and all of our future dealings would occur by letter or in court. I don't like to do that kind of thing. But it happens with ever-increasing frequency, because there are more and more people out there who do not know how to engage in polite, civil conversation about matters as to which they disagree.

Some of them, like the lady attorney, obviously believe that they gain something by conducting themselves like jerks. They are mistaken.

On that very night at home, "Crossfire" came on TV. The issue being discussed interested me, but everyone was yelling and screaming. It wasn't discussion, it was chaos. After a couple of minutes, I clicked it off. I will not subject myself to that noise, and neither should you. If all of us turn it off, pretty soon the networks will get the message.

I believe in civil, reasoned discussion. I believe people can genuinely disagree, and discuss their differences. I believe our society and our system of government invite those who disagree to express themselves, quietly and in turn, so that ideas and reason prevail over bluster, intimidation and emotion. I believe this world is stressful enough. We shouldn't subject ourselves to jerks who don't know the difference between disagreement and disdain. All of those who don't know the difference should go hang out together. The rest of you, come with me. We'll talk and use our manners.

The Story of the Little Christmas Fox

MY MOTHER and her sisters were born to German immigrant parents who settled in Evansville. My Grandpa Greif (rhymes with "wife") had a tailor shop where he made fine clothing for the city's monied elite. Grandma Greif had babies. Four boys, then five girls.

The five Sisters-Greif and two of their brothers remained in town after they married. The five girls were tightly bonded. If one of them was stung by a wasp, the other four could feel the pain – or so it seemed. Their interaction and communications never stopped. My early years were filled with frequent large family gatherings scheduled, orchestrated and choreographed by the Sisters-Greif. Attendance at these affairs was not optional.

The individual Sisters-Greif were wonderful mothers, incredible cooks, fiercely devout Catholics and the objects of great affection from their respective spouses. The combined and allied Sisters-Greif were another story. Their collective wrath could be considerable. Their husbands also shared a special camaraderie, born in no small part of the necessity for their own common self-defense. The sisters' alliance worked kind of like NATO. Any real or imagined infraction against marital bliss, no matter how slight, committed by any one of their husbands, was treated as an attack upon all of the sisters. In times of such trouble, the husband under siege sought refuge and safety in the protective shadows of his brothers-in-law. Their bravery was considerable when they were together and even greater after a few beers. In other circumstances, that is, when they were totally sober and not together, they were no match for the Sisters Greif. Consequently, the husbands conspired together, socialized together, committed minor marital offense together and navigated countless marital skirmishes together. Their friendship was unconditional.

Only once, however, did all five husbands encounter the anger of all of their wives at the very same time and place, and for the very same reason. But out of that occasion, a Christmas story was born.

This particular Christmas Eve was bitter cold. The Sisters-Greif had decreed that they and their families would gather for a Christmas Eve meal at the home of their sister, Marie. Their husbands, who always spent Christmas Eve afternoon "socializing" together, were duly advised to arrive at Marie's house for dinner no later than 5:30 p.m. The plan was that, after dinner, each family would hurry home for its own separate gift-opening. That would leave adequate time for everyone to make it to Midnight Mass.

The sisters and their children were all gathered in Marie's house and ready for a festive meal at 5:30 p.m. that day. But nary a husband was in sight. By 6 p.m., the Sisters-Greif were discussing matters far removed from Christmas cheer and kisses. By 6:30, they were as menacing as Marley's ghost; and still, there was no husband on the premises.

Snow was falling and the ice was thick outside, but those conditions were mild compared to the sisters' icy reception when their husbands finally showed up at about 7 o'clock.

My cousins and I immediately saw that our dads were much jollier than usual. Uncle Charlie, Uncle Gene and my Dad were singing as they came through the door. Uncle Chet had a cigar going, and Uncle Lud, ever the quiet and dignified one, wore a beaming smile but spoke not a word. They were the very picture of Christmas cheer. And their moods didn't change, even in the face of their wives' hushed but unrelenting verbal assaults.

With teeth clenched and hands on hips, they said things like this: "Where have you been, Eugene?" "How could you do this, Charles?" "These kids have been driving us crazy, Chester." "I've never been this mad, Vincent." I had never heard any of these women address their men by their true Christian names. But none of the husbands even flinched. In the Christmas tradition, my dad's eyes twinkled and his voice was merry, as he began to explain to my mom.

"We started with some eggnog in Chet's office downtown," he said. "Charlie, Gene and I got there first.

When Lud came in, he told us he had just seen a little red fox sitting in the front yard of Trinity Cathedral's rectory. None of us believed him, but he just kept talking about that fox. So, at 4:30, when it was time for us to leave, we all walked with Lud back toward his car at the K of C."

The "K of C" was The Knights of Columbus, a Catholic men's club where all of them were members. It was directly across Court Street from the Trinity rectory. Whiskey and other such stuff was served at the K of C.

My uncles were all telling their wives the same story at the same time. "It was windy and snowing and so cold," my dad was saying. "My nose and face were numb from the short walk. Then, just as we crossed Court Street, Lud pointed to the fox. And there it was, right in the middle of the manger scene on the bishop's lawn. It was sitting very still and leaning over the manger, right by the statue of Joseph."

"So," he said, "we all went into the K of C to drink a toast to that little fox that had come to visit the Baby Jesus. Then we bundled up to leave, because we knew it was time for dinner."

"But as we came out of the door, the fox was still there, in the same place, standing so still. Lud's car was parked very near to it and, of course, we didn't want to disturb the fox, so we went back inside for a while. And since it is Christmas, and the fox was warming the Baby Jesus, we raised our glasses one more time to that fox. Then we bundled up to leave again."

"Lo and Behold, when we came out the door," my dad said, "that fox hadn't moved. So we slowly walked together across the street toward the manger scene. Still the fox didn't move. His nose was right over the manger where the little statue of the Christ Child was laying. Now Lud moved slowly ahead, toward his car, but he never took his eyes off of the fox. Then, suddenly, Lud stood straight up, and he walked right over to the fox and picked him up. That fox was frozen solid, sitting right there next to the manger."

"We decided it was a miracle that the fox had died trying to keep the manger warm, and we thought we should have one more Christmas drink in honor of that blessed fox. So we did. It was a Christmas experience none of us will ever forget."

All of my uncles finished their stories about the same time as my dad. But the Sisters-Greif were not buying it. Their silence was evidence of that. But our dads just kept smiling.

Uncle Lud had left the room but, in only a few seconds, he came back in with the little red fox in his arms. It was still frozen, and he sat it down right in the middle of the floor. The wives screamed, my cousins and I squealed, and there were hugs all around. The Sisters-Greif were so shocked by the fox that they began to laugh. Their husbands had encountered such a wondrous Christmas adventure, so they forgot all about the drinking part and forgiveness was immediate. And after all, it was that special time of year.

The dinner that followed may have been the best Christmas Eve event of my life. The little frozen fox had rescued the holiday, and everybody was talking about him at the table.

I was a choirboy at St. Anthony's Church, so I had to arrive earlier than the rest of my family for Midnight Mass. Only my dad and I were in the car as we drove toward the church that night. I begged him to show me where he and my uncles had found the fox. It was only a few blocks out of the way, so he took me down to Court Street, and pointed to the yard under the bishop's office window.

I was puzzled as we passed. "Daddy," I said, "I don't see a manger scene there." My dad just smiled and put a finger up to his lips. And we never discussed the matter ever again.

Every Christmas Eve, I and many of my cousins recall for those who will listen the Christmas of the Little Red Fox, the carefree merriment of our dads, and the spirit of the season they combined to create. The purity of their lighthearted arrival and its "Don't Sweat the Small Stuff" effect upon the Sisters-Greif will live on as we pass the story to our children and the generations that follow.

Merry Christmas.

The Story of Witch Hazel

IN THE NEIGHBORHOOD where I grew up, there were one or two empty lots where we could play baseball until the owners chased us off. I never could understand why they did that. They would talk ugly and threaten to call the cops if we stayed. So, when that happened, we would leave quietly, knowing that soon, in the still of some night, we would have our revenge.

I remember my favorite childhood act of revenge with great pride, and with affection for my comrades. When revenge was in order, we would always discuss it in our secret clubroom. The clubroom was in a combination carriage house and stable that my grandpa had built sometime around 1900. There was a room in there where coal had been stored in the past. Its walls were black with decades of coal dust. The door had been nailed shut sometime before I was born. The only entrance was a two foot square door about five feet off the ground on the alley side of the building where, in years past, the coal truck driver had shoveled in a new load. That was the entrance to the clubroom. No self-respecting adult would climb through that door, and we all knew it. We were safe there.

One old lady always chased us off her property in the bottom of the sixth when the bases were loaded and there were two outs and the score was tied. Her timing convinced me she understood baseball and hated little boys. I called her "Witch Hazel." Witch Hazel knew my mom and dad.

Every time Witch Hazel chased us from her property, she would immediately go inside and call my mother to say I'd been trespassing again. And then I would be punished. My mom said Witch Hazel was a nice old lady who just wanted to be left alone, and we should do so. I was about eight years old. I tried to explain to my mom that when we were playing baseball on Witch Hazel's stupid empty lot, we most certainly were leaving Witch Hazel alone, but that Witch Hazel would not cooperate in our effort to leave her alone, and in fact, it was Witch Hazel who would not leave us alone. Mom wasn't interested in view of the problem.

My dad understood perfectly. I could tell. He didn't like Witch Hazel either, and probably remembered a contest with her counterpart twenty or so years ago. But I know now that he had decided early on that a baseball venue issue wasn't worth an argument with his lady. So he stayed out of it.

As it happened, Witch Hazel had her front porch rebuilt that very summer. In place of the rickety old wood porch, there was now a porch of solid concrete. When the work was finished, she had new metal chairs and a red metal glider delivered so she could enjoy the summer air with her other witch friends. Everything on that porch was washable, durable and fireproof. Well, almost everything.

So it happened that, one particular summer day, Witch Hazel came screaming out of her house when I was up to bat. She was screaming something about having just been through this yesterday and that we all should be in jail and we soon would be because the police were on the way and we were exactly the kind of kids who ought to go to "reform school" and to get off of her property and don't ever come back and so forth and so on.

My friends and I scattered to the four winds and then met in the clubroom. We were mad. For Pete's sake! We'd just been through this yesterday. Didn't this lady know that baseball was America's game and that this was America and that boys who were playing baseball should be left alone? We decided she must be a communist, but whatever she was, this had to stop.

We agreed that we should report her to President Eisenhower, who was very influential and who also hated communists in those days, but we didn't know his address. So we conspired and plotted and planned that whole day. We would teach Witch Hazel to leave us alone with our baseball games, even if it caused us to be grounded the rest of the summer.

There were a lot of evil plans discussed. If a couple of them had taken root, we probably would have gone to the electric chair, or at least to jail, just like Witch Hazel wanted. But cooler heads prevailed, and we settled upon a non-lethal strategy.

We took my old red wagon from the garage and spent much of the rest of the day in the back yard of my friend, Robert. Robert had three big dogs. Both of his parents were gone. We cleaned up Robert's back yard really good that afternoon. Every surviving pile that had been deposited in Robert's back yard by his dogs was now in my wagon. We covered our collection with grass – kind of.

There was a corner grocery store about two blocks away. The owner was my friend, so when I asked him if I could have some small paper bags, he said I could have as many as I wanted. I only took ten the first time, but I went back a few minutes later and got twenty more.

The hard part was lifting the wagon up and passing it through the small clubroom door without spilling its cargo. I can't remember how exactly we did that, but we did.

In the privacy of the clubroom, we transferred the droppings from Robert's big dogs into the small brown bags and closed the top of each one. They looked just like school lunches. We had to work fast because it smelled really bad in there. To make it worse, one kid threw up. When we got all the stuff in the paper bags, there were about twenty-five sacks of dog doo-doo in the wagon. We left this weapon of mass destruction in the clubroom – until after dark.

On summer nights in the early 1950's, we were allowed to play in the neighborhood for a while after dark.

There was no TV, no air conditioning and no concern about the safety of the kids running free in the early evening. Our parents would visit with neighbors on their front porches and we would play games somewhere nearby. Often, the game was "hide and seek," which was a perfect diversion for our plot.

My Uncle Charlie lived right across the street. He smoked and had one of those old Zippo lighters which he fueled with lighter fluid. I knew where Charlie kept his lighter fluid. I also knew he and my aunt would be sitting with my parents on our porch that night because they always did. I even knew what brand of beer my uncle and my dad would be drinking. So while Robert and two others got the wagon out of the clubroom, I "borrowed" Uncle Charlie's lighter fluid. Book matches were plentiful in those days, usually compliments of a funeral home.

The wagon, the matches and the lighter fluid all met in the high bushes next to Witch Hazel's house. Someone – I can't remember who – poured lighter fluid on all those paper bags. And someone – I swear I don't know who – very quietly put those nasty soaked paper bags in five neat piles on Witch Hazel's porch. And someone – I take the fifth amendment – put lighted matches very near those nasty soaked paper bags so as to cause them to ignite and to smell ferociously bad. And then all of the someone's ran very fast away into the night and continued their game of hide and seek.

My mom and dad and uncle and aunt said it was an awful sight. And they couldn't understand why the firemen and police were laughing so hard. Witch Hazel had run out onto her new concrete porch and she had stomped and stomped on those burning paper bags to put out the fires. She had ruined her new house slippers and her porch was a terrible smelly mess. Luckily, the only thing that burned up on the porch was Witch Hazel's new cardboard sign she had just bought that day. It said "No Trespassing – Keep Off."

My mom said she was really glad I had been playing where she could see me when all that happened or she would have thought for sure I had something to do with that trash fire on Witch Hazel's porch. I said I was glad too. My dad didn't say anything. He couldn't because he was laughing too hard. And Uncle Charlie never asked what happened to his can of lighter fluid.

It's All About Relationships

FIRST, we all must tend to the basics: food, clothing, shelter, health care for ourselves and our children – that sort of business. But beyond the basics, there must be some greater reasons we're here. Reasons that make it worth all the trouble.

Consider what the human race has accomplished despite, or in some cases because of, the wars, the plagues, the wilderness, the pestilence, the madmen, the disasters and other obstacles that have been overcome. Our instincts tell us that the events comprising human history could not have occurred entirely by accident. Something big is going on here, something much bigger than the sum of its parts. Bigger than we will ever understand. Our race is on a long journey to somewhere or something beyond our comprehension. I firmly believe that.

We do it like an eternal relay team, constantly passing the baton from generation to generation. It is a never-ending journey, lost in the present and searching for a tomorrow we will not know. In a universal sense, that quest is a purpose we pursue together, each contributing our own very small part.

You and I are here for only a tiny piece of the trip. Even en masse, we who live today are not very significant measured against those who have come and gone and those who will follow. But there are other measures.

Our unique intellects, our sense of place and individuality, tell us we each have a more personal reason for being here. Religion and its promise of a separate spiritual existence aside, there is something we all experience that defines our purpose. It is the combination of our relationships with those we love and with our world. Taken together, the relationships we experience as we live and work give focus and meaning to the present and leave us with a clear benchmark for judging how well we have used the time we have been given.

We all have different talents. That diversity helps us each find a way, a role, that permits us to serve the greater good while we support ourselves. Our complementary talents, therefore, contribute to both the individual and to the whole.

Some devote more time to the common good than others and, consequently, have fewer moments for more intimate experiences. It can never be said that every life will find a balance between the two. But the world, itself, does. In the end, for every moment of personal relationships we sacrifice to our work, there is a moment devoted to our relationships with all humanity. And there seems always to be the correct mix of each.

So, whether we are achievers or survivors, whether we are male or female, and no matter our purpose in life, we are all the same in this: In whatever we do, from the womb to the grave, we all continuously create relationships with those we love and with the larger world. So the richness of our individual time on this planet, and our contributions, however small, to the larger good of the world we live in, are the measures of the relationships we create and foster. In its most naked sense, that is what life is all about. Those relationships. Nothing else survives our trip from the womb to the grave. Treasure them.

You don't choose your family. They are God's gift to you, as you are to them. – Desmond Tutu, *Address, Cape Town, South Africa (Sept. 7, 1986)*

Happy Holidays

Evansville Courier & Press
Sunday, December 17, 2000

SO. THE HOLIDAYS are here. "Peace on earth. Goodwill to men." Right? I can't remember right now. It's something like that.

It is Thanksgiving Day and I am in Arizona. Out of touch with the issues of the day. My mind is at rest from all things unpleasant. But it isn't to last. Reality takes no vacations.

I'm at the deli counter at an "upscale" chain that specializes in organically grown foods that are supposed to be better for our general physical health. The place is also supposed to be staffed by a kinder, gentler sort. It is twenty minutes until closing time; but several customers are still milling about, making their selections.

As I wait for the deli clerk to fill my order, I notice the woman with long silver hair who I'd passed on the way into the store. She is twenty feet away, staring in our direction. Her dark Native-American skin contrasts with her striking hair pulled into a pony tail. She had drawn my attention as I passed her earlier, but now what I see is her sad, pained expression.

I pay for my purchase, turn, and she is gone. But as I walk outside, she's there, standing alone on the sidewalk. And there are tears in her eyes. I ask if she needs help, fully expecting her to say that she has too little money to pay for the food she wants to buy. But money is not her problem.

In the broken English of a Mexican-American, she tells me she came into the deli just before I did, and she asked the same clerk who served me to prepare a container of the same food that I had bought. The clerk had told her that the deli counter was closed and that he would not fill her order. Then she had seen him serve two other customers and then me. I remember those other customers. The only difference is that we are all white and she is not.

She says, between sobs, that she's a good person. She has a job cleaning rooms at a local hotel and she voted in the election. She says she has money to buy her family's food and she wanted to treat them to a special salad with their Thanksgiving dinner. She says she drove far out of her way after working today to come to this store just to buy that salad. But the man won't serve her. What she doesn't say is that an insensitive, ignorant, jerk salesclerk has badly wounded her self-esteem, robbed her of her dignity and ruined her holiday. And what she doesn't need to say is that nothing could be said or done to change that.

I think about going back into the store and demanding that she be served, or maybe giving her my purchase, but as soon as the thought comes to mind I know that would only make things worse. Besides, the "upscale" market doesn't deserve her money. And that's what I tell her. To take her business elsewhere. And, I decide that I'll do the same.

There is no happy holidays ending to this story. She drives away in a very old car, still with tears in her eyes. She will have a lousy holiday, because she isn't white. Thanks to the misguided jerk salesclerk, who thinks that dark skin somehow renders a person undeserving of common courtesy.

I have particular affection for dark-skinned people. A couple of them live in my house and call me Daddy. One of them is a Mexican child whose skin is a shade darker than the lady's. The other is from Brazil and will look a lot like that lady someday. As I drive away, I begin to imagine what my reaction would have been if I had sent one of my kids into that store only to endure the same indignities. What I imagine isn't pretty.

A few days later I'm home again in Indiana. A colleague remarks upon the glut of charity appeals that always arise this time of year but are otherwise scarce. The newspapers and the airwaves and the pulpits are filled with the customary holiday appeals. The Santa Clothes Club. Salvation Army. Toys for Tots. Needy families in our parishes. A family burned out of its home. A sick child who needs a special Christmas trip or an operation. And we respond. As well we should. They are all good causes. But for whom do we respond? Why do we do this only in mid-December and then deride the poor for not working and for taking our welfare money the other 350 days of the year? Why do we do that? I will tell you why.

We do that because during this particular season, we want to feel goodwill, whatever that is; and during the rest of the year we want to feel superior. We want to feel in these few days that we are giving, charitable people. And we know we won't feel very much goodwill as long as there are all those street people and poor families and hard luck stories out there. And all those kids who need a coat or a toy or both. We know that we have so much and they have so little, or nothing at all. And we don't want to be bothered by that. So we give them something, and we feel good that we did. And we guess that's goodwill. But their desperate circumstances must be their fault, because it certainly isn't ours, just like skin color isn't anybody's fault.

So when the Christmas yard lights are out there, many of us seek to excuse our holiday excesses by giving a tuppence or two to some good cause. "Feed the birds, tuppence a bag." So goes the song. And that tuppence given makes us feel so much better. "There," we say. "Now they can have a hot meal on Christmas. And now they can have a coat to wear the next day, when they will have no hot meal. Now, maybe the media will stop the "poor folks" stories, at least for a while. Now we can get on with our holiday. Yeah, that's much better." And it was only tuppence.

But where are we with our tuppence and our strong voices when those people need our help during the other

350 days of every year? Where are we when a black man is racially profiled or when a Mexican worker is paid half the going wage? Where are we then? And where are all of us "good people" when a family of eight lives in two rooms with no air conditioning and eats subsistence food in the heat of the summer? Where are we then?

We may as well be behind that deli counter in Arizona. There's only one difference really. The guy in Arizona makes no bones about it. He's an unkind redneck and doesn't hide it. Many of the rest of us think we're better than him. But we're really only better at fooling ourselves during the holidays and hiding our heads in the sand the rest of the year. It only costs tuppence.

Maybe the best gift we could each give ourselves this holiday is an unlimited supply of compassion and the wisdom and courage to use it. Maybe then we'd come to know true goodwill. Oh, I remember now. It goes like this: "Peace on earth to men of goodwill."

Being a Dad

The Evansville Press
Wednesday, September 17, 1997

S O MY SON, now you are a father. You're so proud of your baby boy and your new role. You can't help dreaming of what this wonderful child will be one day. This is a special time in your life, these first days as a father. A time to celebrate. But when the celebration is over, remember this: What your little boy needs from you the most is for you to be his dad. There are lots of fathers, son. Everybody has one. There aren't near as many dads.

I've often wondered why it is that, in all of the schooling we give our children, no effort is made to teach them how to be parents. You've learned math and science and how to read. You've learned languages and geography and personal health and history. But no school ever gave you a single lesson on parenting, even though being a dad is the single most important thing most men will ever do. Very strange, don't you think? So I will try to tell you.

To be a dad, I mean a real dad, is the most heroic thing a man can ever do. There are no cheering crowds to watch it happen. There are no news stories that report the progress, the successes, the failures, the crises, the fears, the pain, the worries or the victories. A dad does his work mostly out of the view of others. Most often he creates the good times and suffers the hard days in silence. Only he and his family will know about or remember them. But a real dad, in most cases, gives more lasting benefit to our world than any man whose name makes the news for good deeds done.

To be a dad is to be the molder and sculptor of a new person. Real dads work hard at that. And their children remember. Men who are only fathers just let it happen. And their children remember too.

Whether your child has a dad or a father, he will, like every other child, grow and change and learn every day, either for good or ill. And one day this child, who now knows so little and is so dependent, will have to use the life-tools you give him to take and hold his place in this difficult world all by himself. If he is to honor you in his adulthood, you must honor him in his childhood. In large measure, he will grow to be precisely what your efforts make him. That is why, if your dreams for him are going to come true, you can't just be his father. You've got to be his dad.

You can't be a dad every once in a while, son. You can only be a dad if you do it every day. You can't just show up for the fun times, or for the awards, or when it's convenient, or when you can work it into your busy schedule. You have to be a dad first. Always. Every minute. Everything else comes after that. Everything. All the time. You have to be there when he's happy and when he's not. You have to be there when he needs you and when he doesn't. When he's sick and when he's healthy. You must be there.

If you're going to be his dad, you will have to watch him, listen to him and know him better than he will ever know himself. You will be his protector, playmate, comforter, lullaby singer, chauffeur, confidant, censor, entertainer, coach, teacher, biggest fan, sternest critic, best friend, battery mate, drill sergeant, provider, counselor and more. And if you're gonna be his dad, you'll do all you can to be all of those things every day.

Now here are some of the hard parts of being a dad. First, you have to do this job without smothering your child. You have to do much of it without letting him know you're doing it, which becomes more and more difficult as he grows. That means you have to learn to be almost invisible, part of the scenery, and still be effective.

Second, to be a dad, you have to be willing to let go of your child bit by bit, even as you work your love into him and even as your heart tells you that you never want this job to end. Every day, from the very beginning, he has to grow a little, move a little more toward the world and just that much more away from you. And you must let him do that. So that one day you can watch him walk out the door all by himself with the confidence that he can do whatever he needs to do without your help.

You will make some mistakes along the way. Everyone does. Just be sure you recognize a mistake when you make it. And he'll let you down some time or another. All kids do. Be stern with him, but don't give up when those things happen. Just remember those days and do what you must to keep them from happening again.

Some men who would be dads make the same mistakes over and over again because they don't realize they are mistakes at all. Breaking a promise to a child is a big mistake for a dad, son. Don't ever do that. And leaving it to mom to play your role is another big mistake. She knows how to be a mom. A lot of moms are forced by circumstances to try to be dads, too. But moms can't be dads, son, no matter how hard they try. The moms who have had to try know that better than anybody else.

Don't ever hurt your child. That is the worst mistake of all. Dads don't need to do that. There's a much easier and more effective way to discipline a child. All you have to do is gain and keep your child's love and respect. If your boy loves and respects you, if you are his dad and not just his father, you can discipline him with words alone. On the other hand, if you hit your child, two bad things will happen. First, you will hurt him. Second, he will conclude that it's okay for him to hit too. So he'll hit his siblings, his playmates and, eventually, his own child. But, if you don't hit, he won't either.

Oh, just one more thing, son. Maybe it's the most important thing of all. Don't ever pass up an opportunity to hug your boy and tell him that you love him. It's more than okay for a dad to do that. It's essential.

The Party

I WILL GO TO MY GRAVE without understanding how I allowed the story I am about to tell to become a true story. Nevertheless, it did become true and, I guess, it was my fault. Okay, okay. It was my fault.

But first I must tell you this: I was a very good boy when I was in high school. I swear I was. I was in the choir at church and I was in the men's glee club at school. I was up at 4:30 every day to deliver the local morning newspaper to a hundred customers' porches, and I played on the Football, Basketball and Golf teams. And I didn't ever get arrested for anything. I didn't have a fast, fancy car either. I was a certifiable nerd. I was a nerd who could play ball. I really was a good boy . . . except for this one time . . . and I swear I don't know how it happened. But it did happen and it was not good.

Other than the event I am about to recount, the worst moment I remember during all of my high school days was when I made a basket for the opposing team at the beginning of the second half of a sectional tournament basketball game. I forgot that the teams changed baskets after the first half ended. We lost that game by 1 point. My brain just quit working. That also will have to be my excuse for what I am about to describe.

It came to pass in the early summer of 1959 that my parents planned to travel out of the city. They would be gone for about 10 days. This had never happened before and required a great amount of planning for child care.

I was a few months past my 16th birthday, soon to be a junior in high school and the oldest of 4 children. I had a morning paper route in the neighborhood where we lived. I also worked part-time as a dish-washer at a local drive-in restaurant where "car hops" served food to people in their cars. When business was slow, the manager at the drive-in would make me put on a clown outfit and a stupid-looking wig and I would have to ride an over-sized tri-cycle around the drive-in entrances to try to attract business. For doing that I was paid 55 cents an hour. My jobs required that I remain in the house while my parents traveled.

My mother had 4 sisters. They all lived within a few miles of our house. One of them, Aunt Jo, lived only a block and a half away with her husband, Charlie. Jo and Charlie were like a second set of parents to me. Arrangements were made for my younger sister and brothers to stay with the other aunts. Jo and Charlie were to "keep an eye" on me, and, because I was so trustworthy, I would stay alone in our family home and have two meals a day with Aunt Jo.

However, my Dad, a very tall, trim and strong man with whom I did not mess, made it crystal clear to me that I was to stay alone in the house, and he fully expected me to "behave like an adult." The final instructions from my dad went something like this: "David, do not screw this up, and do not let anyone come in our house." That is exactly what he said - more than once. In fact, that might have been buried somewhere in the final farewell before Mom and Dad drove away.

To my great misfortune, all those warnings were for naught. On one or more evenings just before my parents' departure, some super-stupid kid who looked a lot like me and drove around in my jalopy and was a friend of the same bunch of guys as I was, let it slip out of his mouth and into the teenage public domain that David's parents would soon be leaving town for a while. Why that person, who looked so much like me and, in fact, <u>was</u> me, disclosed that information to anybody at all, much less, this group of wayward teens whose tendency to party and drink beer whenever and wherever they could was well-known (one could say, "legendary") throughout the city, remains a mystery to this day. It was also the stupidest thing I have ever done.

So, I well-knew, even before my parents had left the city limits, that the word was out to just about every high school student on the east side of town that, in celebration of the temporary absence of his parents from the city, David was having a "small" BYOB party at his house on Friday night. And everybody was invited. Everybody.

It made no difference whatsoever (and I recall this vividly) that I told everybody who would listen again and again that nobody would be allowed in the house and that the party would be only in the backyard. I also said that only "about 50" kids could attend. As Friday approached, I was very nervous about all this, but there was a quality of the inevitable about it now. There was no turning back.

I had never thrown a teen party before, and I didn't have any money to buy snacks or anything like that, so I didn't do much to prepare for the party. We had six aluminum lawn chairs that I put out in the yard, but that was about it. I didn't worry with the inside of the house, because nobody would be going in there. Right? No. Not right.

I did think ahead enough to assure that three big, strong all-state football players I hung around with planned to be there. They each said they would be there and help me keep everybody in line. With that I thought I had security and order covered. I was wrong about that, and about a lot of other things. Not just a little wrong . . . off the charts wrong.

By 9:30 on Friday night, the "about 50 or so" kids had multiplied like the loaves and fishes of the Bible. And they just kept coming. By 10:30 there were over 400 teenagers partying on, in and around my parents' house. There were cars parked as far away as 3 city blocks, including smack-dab in front of Aunt Jo and Uncle Charlie's house.

The normally quiet streets of my neighborhood were crammed with bumper to bumper traffic and with cars parked every-which-way. They were parked on lawns, in front of driveways and, in some cases, taking over the driveways of several homes. Bedlam quickly developed.

Every bedroom in the house was occupied by teens I had never seen before, all engaged in debauchery. And others were waiting their turns. Drunk teens were spilling beer and dropping cigarette ashes on the rugs and the hardwood floors. My parents' house, in which no smokers lived, was filled with smoke to its rafters. The noise, both inside and outside, was deafening. I watched helplessly as this disaster unfolded and wondering where I would live after my Dad threw me out. I remembered his words: "Don't screw this up." My football star security force was part of the mob.

Mercifully, the first police arrived at approximately 11 p.m. Soon there were about twenty police cars surrounding the block. The boys in blue were herding fleeing teenagers back into my backyard, so they could be identified and checked for sobriety. The few sober kids were sent on their way. The "somewhat drunk" were seated on the ground in the front yard for as long as it took for the booze to wear off. I was ushered into the backseat of one of the police cars where I was asked to provide names of the kids who were too drunk or distraught to speak. There were at least 25 or 30 in that condition. They all received a free ride to the city jail.

I sat in that police car for about two hours providing names, if I knew them, and watching teenagers throw up on the front lawn. By 1 a.m., everyone was gone except the Police Captain, who knew my Dad well from boyhood days, and my Aunt Jo and Uncle Charlie. I kept trying to explain to the Captain how this was not my fault, and that I was a victim here. The Captain provided no comfort to me. None.

I had not consumed any beer all night. I realized early on that the neighbors would soon call the cops and this affair would come to no good end. I had been present at similar events and history was a good teacher. I did not like the taste of beer then and I don't like it now. I was a nerd. I told you that earlier. Most nerds walked away from these parties unscathed because there were always more than enough smart-mouthed non-nerds to keep the police occupied. In this case, the Captain knew I still had the wrath of my parents to face, and that I would have six or seven days to worry about that. So, in the end, I was not arrested.

When I walked back into the house that night and saw the devastation, the death penalty did not seem out of the question. I knew my dad pretty well. Perhaps because he was so tall and fit and muscular, he was careful to manage his anger when I would get out of line. I was not at all sure he could or would do that this time. The house resembled a train wreck, and my parents' bedroom was the point of impact.

Seeing all the damage made me physically ill. Cigarette butts were everywhere. Some of them had been dropped while still burning. Some had fallen onto the hand-braided, hand-sewn wool rugs that lay over the hardwood maple floors throughout the house. My dad had painstakingly handmade those rugs to go with the authentic 18th century antique furniture pieces which he had personally refinished for use in the family house. The antique pieces and the handmade rugs were valuable. Dad was very proud of those rugs and antiques. The mess looked hopeless that night. I knew I could not rehabilitate two of those rugs. Several walls had holes where a fist had gone through them. What was that all about?

The mattress from my parents' bed lay on the floor. Beer had been spilled on it. The master bath looked like it was lifted out of a truck stop. Apparently several guys had held a long-distance shooting contest and nobody won. The other bathroom in the house, upstairs where my siblings and I slept, was a similar mess, but that venue was too small to host a pissing contest.

As I passed through the master bedroom the first time, I heard a very soft moan, a sound like an injured house pet would make. It came from the direction of the antique bed frame. After I looked at the master bath, I went back through that bedroom. There was no sound this time, but I looked under the bedframe, and I found the source of the moaning noise. It was the barely-alive body of one of my good friends. I won't use his name here. I thought he was dead, but he wasn't. I just left him there. When he finally came out of it the next morning, he told me he wished he was dead.

After tending to my paper route at about sunrise, I walked through the house again. I had no idea where to begin or who to call on for help. I began aimlessly picking up the trash, beer cans and cigarette butts. I had no idea for how or in what sequence to clean the place, and I didn't know what cleaning materials to buy. I only knew there was a totally wrecked house to clean up and the buck stopped with me. It was going to be an immense challenge for a sixteen-year-old who knew nothing about housecleaning. But later that day, a miracle took place.

I had four friends whose stay-at-home mothers loved me like they loved their own. Their boys told them about the party and my predicament. They had obviously conferred, because they appeared, one by one, with cleaning supplies at the ready, on the afternoon of the first post-party day. They directed me and worked beside me each day for a week. Aunt Jo helped too. I still refer to those five women as the "Angel Mothers." I swear I have never worked so hard in my life as I did the next six days and nights, but the effort paid off.

Thanks to the Angel Mothers, by the time my parents pulled into the driveway, Humpty-Dumpty was back together again. Even the stale beer and cigarette smells were gone. Except for a stray cigarette butt my Mom would find from time to time during the next few weeks, there was no evidence that The Party had ever occurred. For that, my parents were forever grateful. But Mom had been through a week of hellish worry, believing she would return to a trash-heap of a house, and at the same time, her pride in me was at an all-time low. My Dad, in addition to some very heavy work responsibilities during the trip, had to bear the entire daily brunt of Mom's anxiety and anger. And he knew precisely who to blame.

Worse yet, although I wouldn't know about it until several years later, there was one more very bad unspoken consequence of my poor judgment. News of The Party had spoiled for my parents a long-anticipated 20th wedding anniversary trip. The mood of the trip was forever altered when they heard from Aunt Jo about The Party. Truth be told, to this day, I shall regret that consequence. I cannot count the number of times I apologized to them even after I had grown children of my own. But this memory gave me pause to control my own temper when my children did equally stupid things.

So here is the final chapter. My mother did not speak to me for several days. She left the matter of punishment entirely to my Dad. She was so grateful to her sister and the Angel Mothers for doing the remediation work that she included them in her night prayers for the rest of her life. My dad was in control and non-violent, a development I attribute entirely to the Angel Mothers who told him how hard I worked to get the house back in shape before he and Mom returned. But he did scare the hell out of me, and he issued a punishment he knew I would never forget.

About an hour after their return, my Dad summoned me to the makeshift workshop he maintained in the detached two-car garage that sat at the back of our property. It was hot and dark in there, and nobody else was around. I remember thinking that the death penalty might be preferable to what was about to happen to me. Although my Dad had not laid a hand on me since I was about four years old, I truly expected something involving physical pain. But he didn't resort to corporal punishment. He did say that he had thought about it and decided he loved me too much to do that. But he reminded me very bluntly that he had trusted me not to "screw up" and I had done that in a very big way. He was going to make sure it never happened again. And he did. This was the last time my Dad ever punished me for anything.

Then came the hammers. "No driving for the rest of the summer and you will be in the house every night from 5 p.m. until you get up to carry your papers." I had expected all that. What I did not expect came next. "You, David, are going to paint the entire outside of this house and garage. You will not get any help from anyone. You will use a wire brush and a putty knife to remove all the loose paint, and you will put two coats of fresh white paint neatly on this house from top to bottom. You will start at 8 a.m. every morning and you will work until 4:30 every afternoon except Sundays. You will get 30 minutes for lunch each day and you will start tomorrow. I will be checking your work every day, and if you don't do it right, you will do it over. And by the way, if you don't finish the job before preseason football practice starts, you won't be on the team."

And with that said, my Dad got up, kissed my sweaty forehead, and walked into the house.

I sat in that steamy garage by myself for a while after that, trying to remember how I could have let all this happen. I was unaccustomed to being so stupid. I realized that the seeds for this entire chain of events were sown when some really dumb kid who looked a lot like me mentioned to a group of his buddies a few weeks earlier that his parents were going out of town and that he (the dumb kid who looked a lot like me) would be home alone for several days. Even though I truly didn't know at the time I said it that I was issuing an invitation to a party to every teenager in town, and that most of them would show up with beer, cigarettes and condoms in hand, I certainly should have known all that. What a dumb ass that kid who looked a lot like me was! And yes, he, the dumb ass, was me.

And it never, ever happened again.

Epilogue

There are at least three valuable lessons to be learned from my bumbling fall into stupidity in 1959.

The first is for parents everywhere and their pre-teens and full-fledged teenagers. It is that even good kids, kids with a long history of respectful and responsible behavior, can make very irresponsible decisions with seriously bad consequences. They are, after all, immature people still learning to be adults. When these kids screw up, whether intentionally or not, they know it before anybody else and they usually regret it. One serious screw up does not turn an otherwise respectful and responsible teenager into a lost cause. Tough love may be an appropriate reaction, but branding the child forever an untrustworthy outcast is not. And neither is parental violence.

The second is for anyone who has the responsibility to discipline a teenager whose mistake creates a real risk of injury or property damage. A large number of unsupervised, sexually-active teens drinking, smoking heavily and dropping burning cigarettes all over in a house is a recipe for disaster. My dad knew that, and he also knew that I had not thought about it. And he was right. So, during the lecture he gave me in the garage, he made certain that I understood the dangers the police were responding to when they rushed to The Party: alcohol poisoning, drunk driving, fire, intoxicated kids with weapons, teen love triangles, personal accidents such as falling down a staircase. All of that and more could have happened. We were just lucky that none of them did. The lessons to be driven home by the punishment are as critical to the process as the punishment itself.

And finally, the Third Lesson targets the teenagers who read this. It is a rule to live by that is as old as time itself, and simple to say. Only the exercise of self-discipline will assure that you begin to develop self respect at the earliest possible age. When you are about to do or say something that will put yourself or someone else in danger, or that you know will not please those who love you or that you will later regret, govern yourself. You will be glad you did.

<u>Messages</u>

IN 1991, in the month of March, on a Saturday, I answered a phone call from my friend Robert, a missionary in Brazil. One month to the day after that phone call, my wife and I came back from Brazil with a baby girl. It seems like only yesterday. But today she's grown up and not a child anymore.

We were too busy. Our lives were too frantic and our priorities out of whack. We worked too many hours and took on too much responsibility. Because of that, our family time was compromised, and we missed or hurried through some of the most important moments of our kids' lives. Worse yet, we missed some of the messages they sent us as they grew. Messages that told us how they felt about themselves, about us, and about their world.

Even on those occasions when we took the time to step back and assess our work as parents, it was hard to know how we were doing. Probably because we were looking through the same eyes and thinking with the same brains we used every other day. To get a true picture, we needed regular performance appraisals from the experts.

There came a day, when the little Brazilian was about ten, that she me reminded again, for maybe the twentieth time, that the experts on the matter of how we were doing as parents were with us every day. Depending on their ages, they were either under our feet, in our back seat, or on the phone with their teenage friends. They were the ones who really know. And they were constantly telling us, if we would only listen.

In my home, I was not a very good listener most of the time. There were usually things that my mind couldn't put aside at day's end. My brain was too tired; and it shifted into autopilot. So I didn't absorb as much as I should from conversations about who did what in school today, when the next tumbling lesson was, what happened at the last one, who won't be home for dinner and why. And I did not always sense the changing moods and tones of voice that came with those discussions.

Shame on me. Shame on me, because folded into those conversations were important messages about how and what my children were doing. Whether they were happy, sad, worried or troubled, and why.

I really tried to shift gears and not be preoccupied at those times. But my success rate was low. Looking back, I suspect I'm not the only parent guilty of that sin. And matters have only become more complicated since then. The burdens of the workaday world are heavy, tenacious and play no favorites. So, much of the time, many well-meaning, truly dedicated parents have to be to be hit over the head with blunt, direct information to assure their immediate attention.

So it came to pass that one evening my little gift from Brazil did precisely that. This time, the news was good. She came to me with a short essay she had typed on our new computer. It wasn't an assignment for school, nor was it prompted by anyone else. She just typed it, pasted her picture at the bottom, and brought it to me.

This is what it said, misspellings, grammatical mistakes and all:

"**My dad:** My dad David V. Miller is a lawyer at Ziemer, Stayman, Whitsle and Shoulders. He has supported our family extremely well. I love him very much. So does my whole family. Candy, Eric, Brant, Andrew, Ashley Layne and me Sage D. Miller think that he is an amazing father. He worked very hard to get Layne home from Mexico and to get me home from Brazil. We are adopted. I think he is great. I don't know what I would do without him. I love him very much. By Sage D. Miller"

I guess she put her school picture with it so I'd be sure to know exactly which Sage D. Miller was the author. After wiping back a few tears, I concluded that her words were a pretty satisfactory report card. I've saved that piece of paper in a place where it won't get lost.

In the days that followed, Sage's little essay remained on my mind. I wondered what motivated her to write it. Maybe she thought I needed to be told that she feels pretty good about things these days. So that's what she did. Maybe she knew it would make me feel good. It did. Maybe she thought I should be hit between the eyes with a progress report, because otherwise it wouldn't register. She was probably right. Whatever her motivation, she made me realize that I should have already known how happy and secure she feels. I didn't. But if I'd been listening, I probably would have. So, I resolved again to listen more closely to the conversations and observe more carefully the moods of the occupants in my house. Because if I don't, the next time the news might not be so good.

In the blink of an eye, Sage would be fifteen. I have had a teenage girl in my house once before. They are somewhat different than ten year old girls. As a rule, teenage girls don't often communicate with their daddies about how things are going, much less provide written reports. They just explode in tears at unpredictable intervals.

So one day about five years later, when I was helpless in the wake of yet one more teenage crisis that I didn't understand, I retrieved that old job assessment and read it a few times. That made me feel a little better. Then I handed it to Sage and asked her to give me a written update and a hug.

There are at least two things I've learned during all these years of parenting six children. First: There are some times when all the listening in the world will not help a guy understand what's bothering a girl so it might help if she writes it down and lets me think about it. And second: Hugs from a daddy can make a lot of things better, even when Daddy doesn't have a clue what the problem is.

To Hell and Back

Evansville Courier & Press
Sunday, June 4, 2000

I HAVE TRAVELED to hell and back. Maybe you think the only way to do that is to have one of those "near death" or "out of body" experiences; but that's not true. You can drive to hell if you choose; and after your visit, you can return home, albeit worse for the wear. That's what I did.

Hell exists right here on earth every day, and in numerous locations all at once. Thousands of people (like me) purchase expensive tickets to take themselves and their loved ones into these hellacious places and willingly submit to the suffering that is inflicted there. Even more insane, while they are there, these people (like me) purchase outrageously priced memorabilia to carry home from their encounter with hell.

These various enclaves of hell, like other fugitives from sensible society, operate under different names and move quickly from city to city, sucking money from otherwise good people, including children, teenagers and their ordinarily responsible parents (like me). In all cases, it is a lot of money that could be better-used for feeding the poor, housing the homeless, my pension, driver education and other similarly wholesome pursuits.

These ungodly operations are generically called "rock concerts." The particular species that lured me into the abyss was called a Britney Spears Concert several years ago.

Say what? Who is Britney Spears? How the hell should I know? I was fifty something. But I have this daughter who, at that time, was nine-something; and she was, along with millions of others who had strayed from the righteous path of acceptable musical offerings, in a trance of adoration for Britney. There is no known cure for this affliction except the ageing process. But, as we all know, some people never grow up.

Now Britney was a sixteen-something girl with breast implants already and a very tight, revealing wardrobe. (Which leads me to ask: Britney, where was your mother, child? Where was your father? And didn't you have homework to do?) She sang very loud songs which all sounded exactly the same. My daughter and her friends knew by heart every word of every song that Britney had ever recorded. That amounted to either eleven or twelve words. It depends on whether you think "unh" is a word.

Britney, however, did not perform her concerts alone, oh no! She was assisted by several other similarly misguided (or unguided, your choice) young people who had abandoned all hope and entered the world of rock noise. They, like Britney, suffered from the delusion that they had talent. They apparently believed that removing their shirts and screaming unintelligible words while jumping aimlessly about on a stage in front of twenty or thirty thousand screaming people required talent. It does not. This exercise is called "warming up" the crowd. For those of you who have never been to a rock concert, this is all true. I swear. I saw it with my own eyes.

They are a pitiful lot, these helpers; and, in this case, they were mostly male persons. I won't say "boys," because they came onto the stage wearing funny clothes, either real baggy or unbelievably tight, that real boys wouldn't be caught dead in. They moved wildly about and managed to have coordinated seizures more or less in time with the beat of a more or less inadequate but very loud drummer who worked with a more or less inadequate but equally loud group of guitar and bass players. All of this to heat the place up for Britney.

It is my own personal opinion that Warm-up Group Number One (The Drug Busters) was composed of the same people who later appeared as Warm-up Group Number Two (The New Millennium Slugs). They looked, sounded and gyrated exactly alike.

Here's how it happened. My daughter's ninth birthday was approaching. One night at dinner, we adults in the house made the mistake of asking what she would like for her birthday present. She would soon be nine, so how bad could it be, right? An American Girl doll, maybe. A sleep-over with her friends. But no. It was none of that. What she wanted, she said, was to take a little friend and go to a rock concert. She didn't say which rock concert and I, assuming she meant some event coming to our local stadium, did not ask. I should have asked.

Instead, I said "Sure," she could do that. I thought I'd send her teen-age brother with her, stay up a little later than usual, pick them up when it was over, and I would be done, off the hook. No problem.

But it was a problem; and I wasn't off the hook. Because it was Britney who she wanted to see in concert; and Britney wasn't coming to our town. No, indeed. Britney wasn't even coming close to our town. She and her loud, obnoxious friends and all of their noise-making equipment were going to do their rendition of hell in Cincinnati. And, because I had failed to qualify my promise, I would be there to see it. It could have been worse, I supposed. It could have been London or Hong Kong.

The drive into hell was pleasant and uneventful. The devil has a way, I'm told, of deceiving his victims into a false sense of security while they travel the slippery slope. And so it was with me. I mused as I drove that this Britney concert might even be fun. After all, I told myself, I had never seen a sixteen-year-old with breast implants; and besides, she's just a young girl who sings "pop rock," not that "hard rock" or "heavy metal" stuff. "It probably won't be that bad," I thought. Wrong again.

You'd think a person who spent the 70s, 80s and 90s raising six kids would be more in touch with reality, right? Not me. And it was my own fault. I've hidden from that part of reality, hunkered down with my Sinatra, Denver and Bachrach collections. I took a pass on most of the "music" of the last twenty-five years, because I believe something is terribly wrong with the current world of popular music. It's a wasteland of noise and poor diction. So, I should have known the torture I was in for in Cincinnati. But if I had admitted that to myself in advance, I probably would have chickened out and broken my word to my daughter.

So I walked into hell that night totally unprepared. As we arrived, the "first" warm-up group was just beginning. It consisted of six guys dancing and screaming, telling Cincinnati to "put your hands together," and asking those assembled this earth-shaking question: "Are you ready to party?" The crowd of 25,000, except for me and my wife, appeared to say yes.

The second "warm-up" group consisted of six guys dancing and screaming and insisting that Cincinnati put its hands together yet again. Same noise. Same jumping around for another 30 minutes. At that point, I guess they thought we were "warmed-up."

Then followed the calm before the storm. Britney was in the building, but there were souvenirs to be sold. My daughter chose a T-shirt with a picture of Britney on the front. I paid $30 for it; and we returned to our lofty perch just as the lights went down.

The fanfare blared. The fireworks (I swear!) exploded. And dancers appeared to announce her coming.

I was breathless. I mean, it was so loud I couldn't breathe. And then, suddenly, there she was. Coming up out of a smoking hole in the floor, presumably straight from the real hell. The crowd was screaming. Britney was screaming; her helpers were screaming. The drums and guitars were in there somewhere. Now it was so loud I couldn't hear a thing. My ears were numb. It was a miracle! Me, a faithless reprobate, saved from hell, saved from Britney's noise. But then my hearing returned, and I had a terrific headache.

Britney's noise didn't last very long. I guess it's hard to make up very many songs that all have the same eleven or twelve words. So, before we suffered irreversible ear damage, she was gone and it was over and I was free. The walk back to the hotel was one of the high points of my whole life, because I knew that no matter what else ever happened to me, I would never have to do that again. Unless, of course, I am such a bad person that I get sent to the real hell. This may have been God's final warning to me.

In the end, I guess it was worth it. My daughter had the time of her life; and she wore her t-shirt all the time. And I could return to my beloved Sinatra/Mercer CD. Ahh, there! A little piece of heaven. And so back to my foxhole that protected me from hell. I might never come out again.

My Train Wreck Graduates

MY DAUGHTER, she of the room that resembles a train wreck, graduated from high school today. I watched it happen, but I wasn't really there. I was other places with her, watching her grow.

I was in the hospital the day she was born. Her blue eyes were open with wonder. They did not cry. They just looked back at her mother with a serenity I did not understand.

I was at the front door of Montessori Academy when she was barely two. I remembered her dress, blue and white checked. There was a red ribbon in her hair, her golden red hair, like her mother's. She marched up the stairs to the door in her high-top Stride Rites all by herself and waved goodbye when she got to the top. No tears. She was secure and at peace. And school began. I went to work. Her mother cruised around the block for hours to be sure she didn't wander off. That was only yesterday.

I was at Disney World with her on my shoulders watching the parade. She was three and melted drops from her strawberry ice cream cone dripped into my hair. I didn't care and she didn't either. Mother cared and cleaned her up.

I was with her on Christmas days when there were too many presents and on visits to her grandparents where there were so many hugs and so many cousins. I was throwing her high into the sky at the swimming pool, time after time, until my arms were sore; and she was laughing and begged for one more flight, one more splash.

I was in the wicker rocking chair in her bedroom. It was her bedtime and we were singing together. It was a ritual. Every night. The same songs every night until she fell asleep in my arms. And she was at peace and serene.

I was at a million ball parks trying to watch her brothers play baseball and soccer and keep her safe from harm at the same time. And the birthdays, I remembered the birthdays – swimming parties, family parties, pizza parties, too many presents, too many parties. Sometimes two or three parties per birthday. I worried she would be spoiled. Her mother said not to worry. She would be fine. And she was.

I remembered when she was six and a half, she went to Mexico with us to finalize the adoption of her brother. She was the first one to pick him up at the foster home. She loved him unconditionally and immediately. She was secure and at peace with her place in the family. And that never changed.

I was at the dancing lessons, the piano lessons and recitals and more recitals. Mom spent hours in the car to get her there and back. They were going to all the lessons mothers dream of their daughters taking. Then suddenly, without any warning, those lessons and recitals ended. They turned into soccer practices and softball games. She didn't want to dance anymore. She wanted to run and kick and catch and hit, and so she did. Her mom didn't understand, but again she spent hours and hours in the car to get her there and back. Because even though she didn't understand, she knew how to mold a serene child.

I was telling her to clean her room for the millionth time, knowing all the while that she wouldn't. I supposed it was because she liked living in a train wreck. Mom said just close the door and don't look at it. So that's what we did.

I was pacing the floor when she was out past her curfew, desperately looking out the window for the car bringing her home. And I was always too tired and too relieved to fuss very much when she finally came home. And then I was watching her drive away in her little red car and hoping that if she hit anything it would only be a mailbox – and it was.

I was wishing I could do it all over again with her, and this time really soak up every minute. I'd be there to watch every centimeter of her growth. I would hold her more and teach her more and be at more dance practices and recitals and games and doctors' visits . . . and then they called her name.

She walked across the stage and accepted her diploma, and charged into her future. It was the same confident step that had taken her through the door at

Montessori fifteen years ago. And she was at peace, with the same steady gaze as the day she was born.

I've done this graduation business several times before, but never with a girl. It's different for a dad when it comes to raising a girl. There is a great line from a song in the musical play, "Carousel." "You can have fun with a son, but you've gotta be a father to a girl." I've tried really hard to do my part. But I'll never know if I've done enough.

Not too many fathers understand what goes on in the brain of a female child. I certainly don't. We've never been little girls. Maybe that's why it's so fascinating to watch them grow. Maybe that's why it's so hard to let them go. Most of us, even if we do our best, can only hang around, try to help and try to understand what the hell the current problem is. Then, when this time comes, a dad gets the feeling that he can't possibly be this close to finished with this one. In fact, everything about this girl child of mine reflects her mother's persistence and understanding and dedication. Thank God for her mother. I wished I could have helped more. But more than that, as she walked off the stage, I wished we could do it all over again.

Housebuilding – the Husband's Role

IF A MARRIED MAN wishes his marriage to survive the building of a new house, it is very important that he understands his role in the house building process. From the very first moment of the planning stage until the day after the last subcontractor leaves the site for the last time, the husband must listen very carefully every time his wife explains the options that are available for any particular feature of the house. Then, when she is finished, that is, when the husband is absolutely sure she is absolutely finished, the husband must then say something like, "Whatever you decide to do will be great," or words to that effect. That is Rule Number One.

Now for Rule Number Two. Sometimes the husband will want to visit the construction site. It is very dangerous for a husband to do this without his wife. But some husbands are interested in the general progress of this very expensive undertaking, so they go there on occasion just to kind of look around.

When a husband does this, often there are various workmen present and one or two of them will ask him questions about some detail of the work. These are usually reasonably simple questions like, "Do you want this laundry room door to open inward or outward?" or "Do you want the hardwood floor boards to run east-west or north-south?" or "Where exactly do you want the wall switch for the bathroom exhaust fan?" or "How many electric receptacles do you want, and where do you want them?" These are not life and death matters. They are, however, the stuff that divorce is made of, and the husband must be alert not to screw up when he encounters such situations.

These questions present a double problem to the inexperienced husband who has never built a house with a wife before. On the one hand, he wants the workers to believe that he is authorized to make any necessary decision regarding this structure. After all, he is the man of the house. However, he is likely to forget that the workers have already met his wife, and that they have wives too, and that they know the pecking order. But while the inexperienced husband is trying to figure a way to protect his macho image, he also must remember that he had better let the wife decide what answer to give to these questions, because if he doesn't, he will have two problems – the wife will eat his lunch for giving the wrong instructions, and he will have to pay twice for having the work done, because it will have to be done over.

The safest and most deceptive response that the husband can possibly give to the workers when this situation arises is as follows: "I'll think about that and get back to you later today." Then he must leave the construction site and consult his wife to get the answers. He then must return to the construction site and tell the workers what his wife said to do and try to make them believe that he made the decision. This is a great deal of trouble to endure just to protect your image with a group of tradesmen he probably will never see again for the rest of his life. And it is futile anyway because the tradesmen know exactly what is really going on.

After this happens to a husband four or five times, he will ordinarily decide to level with the workers. "I'll ask my wife and let you know," he will say. Or, "My wife will be here soon, so you can ask her." The workers will be very relieved when the husband adopts this candid approach. They know from experience that husbands do not care about such matters. More importantly, they know who calls the shots and that it is most definitely not the husband. But they play the game with husbands just to be courteous, and then laugh when hubby is gone.

Husbands will discover a great sense of inner peace when they level with the workers. It is a tipping point that causes a bonding effect between them because most construction workers are men and they are husbands too. They understand that most husbands do not care very much where the wall switch is placed. A guy will find it when he needs it. Nor do men often care which way the laundry room door swings; it will open and close either way. And hardwood floors can be walked upon whether the boards run one direction or another. Every man alive knows that. But wives don't think that way. And they do care about such details.

For example, I have seen homes wherein almost every electric receptacle is placed so that it is hidden from view by a piece of furniture that the homeowners didn't have when they decided to build the house. Even if a guy cared to engage in this exercise, for most of them it would be a "chicken or egg" problem. Do you first decide on the placement of the wall receptacles and switches and then select furniture that will hide them, or do you buy the furniture first, taking precise measurements in the process, and then lay out where each piece of furniture will be forever situated in the house so you can then decide where to place the receptacles and wall switches? Not only would most guys not know how to begin such a project, they are not even capable of thinking about such things, and, therefore, would not consider them problems that needed solving in the first place.

Not so for women. They not only knew how important these decisions are, they also knew exactly which decisions to make first and how to mix and match them. And furthermore, after such decisions are made, women never forgot any of them. Husbands ordinarily will not, and most of them cannot, do that. But thanks to the females among us, a man of the house might never have to look at another electric receptacle in his house ever again. Imagine that! And he didn't even know they were ugly in the first place. But they must be. The only problem the man of the house then has is finding an electrical outlet when he needs one.

I am told that there are thousands of important decisions like that which go into the proper building of a new house. I just can't imagine what they are.

So if you are a married man and you wish to remain married, and if you and your wife ever decide to build a new house, this advice could save your marriage. You must always listen carefully to your wife when she is telling you about the choices to be made. However, you must always, always, make sure you have a glass of wine in your hand when this occurs. Red or white – it makes no difference. Have a few sips while she is talking and don't interrupt. When you are absolutely sure she is finished, have another sip or two while you pretend you are thinking about the options, and then tell her to do whatever she thinks best. Because that's what is going to happen anyway.

Children

MY YOUNGEST SON, Layne, the fifth of our six children, met me at the door one evening several years ago as I arrived home from work. He gave me his homework assignment sheet from his fourth grade teacher. It said that the student should ask one parent to write a paragraph saying why the child was "special."

I believe every child on this planet is "special." I have felt from the first breath of my adult experience that every birth of every baby is nature's most unappreciated miracle. Like the biblical symbolism of rainbows, each newborn brings with it a measure of new hope and unconditional love to our world. This would be the first homework assignment I ever welcomed in my life because this teacher had wandered into my playground – the Ballpark of the Written Word.

However, there were two problems to overcome. I wanted to expand the topic to cover all children, and then there was that "one paragraph" thing. So, although I couldn't tell Layne, the only solution I could think of was to cheat. By that I mean I just wouldn't exactly follow the instructions. And by that I mean I didn't follow the instructions at all. But the teacher let me get by with it.

Here is what he read, all crammed into "one paragraph."

"Imagine for a moment that you are standing outside on the clearest of nights and you can see all of the stars in the sky. And imagine that while you are looking at all of those millions of beautiful stars, some very bright, some very dim, but all twinkling like diamonds, God speaks to you and says: 'I can tell by the wonder in your eyes and the peaceful expression on your face that you admire my stars and that you would like very much to have one. And I also know that if you had the responsibility for one of my stars you would love it with all of your being.' And then imagine that you answer God and say to Him: 'Oh yes, I would very much like to have one of your stars, and if I did, I would love it and care for it and make sure it showered its light in every direction for all of your creation to enjoy. But I have done nothing to deserve one of your stars.' And then imagine that God says to you: 'It is not for you to decide whether you deserve to have one of my stars. In fact, no one does. But just as you are, each of these heavenly bodies is one of my children, and was created to be loved. So you may have one of my stars upon your promise to love it without condition.' And then imagine that you say to God: 'But how shall I choose one? All of your stars are so precious to my eyes, and they are so different. Some are lighter, some are darker. Some twinkle, some shine and some are soft in their glow. Some are far, some are near. How shall I choose?' And then imagine God says: 'I did not say that you could choose. I said you can have one to love. I will choose. Here. Take this dark star that always twinkles with energy and moves fast around the heavens. This star is now yours to love and to care for, but always be vigilant to guide this star on its path. It is full of fire and curiosity. It will require your constant love and attention.' And then imagine you say: 'Thank you, God. I will name this star Layne. And I promise I will do my best to make you proud of him as he grows. And then imagine that God goes off to place more stars and to make more stars and to do other things that God does. And finally, imagine the night ends, a new day dawns, and God leaves you there to care for and nurture his little star. And from that moment, the little star must find its own way through life with only your care and guidance. That is why Layne and every other child is special. They are, every one, the pure and precious handiwork of God."

One paragraph, just like the teacher said.

Everything's got a moral, if only you can find it. – Lewis Carroll, *Alice in Wonderland, Chapter IX*

Heroes

IT HAS ALWAYS BEEN important to me to have a hero. A hero is somebody you admire—somebody you would like to help do whatever it is that person does even though that person obviously does not need any help.

My first hero was my Uncle Edward. He lived in Milwaukee, and he was very successful in business. I was too young to know how he did it. Come to think of it, I still don't know. All I know is that my mom said he made a lot of money and whenever he came back to Evansville to visit, he came to my house and took me for a ride in this big—I mean really big—black car. He was interested in cameras and always took me to a camera shop on Oakley Street behind the Willard Library.

The Willard Library is where I learned about sex for the first time. No, that's wrong. The Willard Library is where I READ about sex for the first time, because I decided to research the matter thoroughly. It happened after my older friend, Johnny (who was never one of my heroes), showed me a used condom in the park and then made fun of me because I didn't know what it was. I actually LEARNED about sex much later. What I read at the Willard Library was very confusing to my ten-year-old mind. They didn't write any good sex education books for kids in the late 1940s and the early 50s. If they did, the Willard Library didn't own them in 1953. I haven't checked back there since.

The problem is that every time I pick a hero, the hero soon dies. This one summer night, when I was about six, we were driving home from a family picnic. All of my local cousins and aunts and uncles had been there. It had been a great day. We had those kind of picnics several times every summer when I was young. People don't seem to do that much anymore. During the drive home I was wishing Uncle Edward could have been there because I had done something very special that day. I had ridden a two-wheel bike all by myself for the first time. (Training wheels had not been invented yet.) Even so, as I lay dozing in the back seat of the car, I had the strangest feeling that something was not right in my universe. When we got home, the telephone was ringing. It was my aunt who had hosted the picnic. She was my mom's oldest sister, and I thought she was the boss of everything in the family. She thought so too. She was calling to tell my mom that Uncle Edward had "dropped dead." That happened a lot in the late 1940s. People just dropped dead. No further medical explanation was given. So much for Uncle Edward. He had abandoned me in my moment of triumph. Not his fault though. No hard feelings. After a few days, I decided I would just have to find another hero.

It took a while. Heroes don't just hang out everywhere. Then I heard about this great new movie star—James Dean. He was from Indiana. Until that time, I didn't know movie stars were allowed to be from Indiana. Every time his name came up, my mom and some of my girl cousins acted funny. When Mom took me to see "Giant," I was hooked. I wasn't even ten, but James Dean was who I wanted to be. Good looking and wild. I wasn't good at being wild, because Sister Cunegunda (I swear) did not permit wild. It wasn't very long after that when James missed a curve in his new sports car. I was a hero-orphan again. I still believe that the wreck was somehow Sister Cunegunda's fault.

In the sixth grade, I commenced my working life. I agreed to deliver the morning newspaper. There was a downside. Four-thirty A.M. was very early when I was eleven. It still is. Every morning at about 4:30 I had to fold eighty-five papers so I could throw them to (or near) my customers' porches from my bike. It takes a while to fold eighty-five papers at 4:30 in the morning. So I always propped one of the papers up on my kitchen table and read while I folded. I read a column called "Morning Assignment" by Joe Aaron. Joe was pretty funny most of the time. After a while, I began doing my homework assignments in the same writing style as Joe used. The nuns at St. Anthony's did not approve. Joe didn't always write in complete sentences. So I didn't either. They didn't like that. After several Parent-Teacher conferences, followed by an equal number of Parent-Child conferences, I abandoned Joe's writing style, but I never forgot him. The nuns had conspired against me again. By the time I reached the age when I could write in any style I chose, Joe was not among us.

Joe had family in New Mexico. It was a long drive to New Mexico. I remember him writing about a trip he made out there. He had passed a road sign that said some little town was 50 miles away and Santa Fe was 100 miles away. A little later, he passed another sign. It said that he was 30 miles from the little town and 60 miles from Santa Fe. It was at that moment, he said, that he realized that not only was he going to Santa Fe, Santa Fe was coming to him.

When I was about 12, I discovered music. My first musical hero was Glenn Miller. He had been dead since the war, but I liked his music anyway. That, however, did not go over well with my buddies on the St. Anthony football team. My buddies did not like me very much in the first place, and most of them were given to violence. I, therefore, renounced my allegiance to Glenn Miller. I picked Buddy Holly and The Big Bopper as my new favorites. They were pretty good, and they were acceptable to my buddies. I learned to sing "Hello Baby" and "That'll Be The Day," and almost immediately their plane went down.

This was getting spooky. I decided that the heroes of the world didn't need me. I needed them because they were the stuff of ambition. They were goals to reach for. But I was a jinx, so I decided I wouldn't like anybody very much. Then John Kennedy came along. I was seventeen when he was elected and twenty when he was shot. I liked him a lot, and Bobby too, and Martin Luther King. Their messages were my credo back then. Those were my high school and college days. I was idealistic and political. Everybody was. But, as the song says, "I just turned around and they were gone."

I didn't like Richard Nixon very much and he was like a Timex—he just kept on ticking. I didn't wish Richard any bad luck. It just seemed like every person I did admire was doomed the minute I signed on, but my anti-heroes hung around like a bad case of poison ivy.

After the events of 1963 and 1968, I swore I'd never have another hero. I really meant it this time. I wanted one. I needed one. We all do. But I thought I'd better not. I might pick someone the next time the world really needed. I made it through the early 1970s okay. Spiro Agnew didn't appeal to me, and I couldn't understand the lyrics to most of the new music. The bumper stickers said even God was dead. Not much left. I did, however, begin to listen to the music of John Lennon and Elvis Presley a lot in the middle 70s. Goodbye boys—just when I was getting to know you—but I swear, you were never really my heroes. Scout's honor.

There wasn't much to like about the late 70s or early 80s either. Inflation and high interest rates didn't have much personality. Neither did Jimmy Carter or Michael Millkin. I was desperate for someone to admire. One day, in a fit of total boredom, I turned to the editorial page of the newspaper. Lo and behold, there was Lewis Grizzard. What a gem! Could he write, or what?

By the time I began to read him religiously, Lewis was already sick. God had screwed up his heart. He said so himself—Lewis did—in a column. He didn't blame God though. He blamed his daddy who, according to Lewis, failed to get an adequate toehold at the critical moment. When I read that, I knew that Lewis wouldn't blame me if something bad happened to him, because he had already blamed someone else in advance. But I prayed every day for him. He was my hero. I really wanted him to hang around.

It is perfectly normal to aspire to do something well and to admire someone who does. That's the way I had felt about all my heroes, and that's the way I felt about Lewis. I felt like if Lewis and I could ever sit down and talk, I could give him some great ideas that he would then cleverly develop into journalistic masterpieces. Lewis had the only typewriter in the world with a southern accent. I absolutely believe that. I also believe that he took it with him when he left. Lewis lasted quite a while, despite being the object of my admiration. I was careful. I never wrote or called him. But about two months after I went to see him in concert—you guessed it—he checked out, ... on my birthday. What a blow! How absolutely inconsiderate!

A lot of people have died since then, but none of them were my fault, because I have had no hero since then. More than that, I have taken a blood oath that I will do my best never to admire anyone again. And if I do, I won't like them, I won't read their books, I won't go to their movies, I won't watch their speeches on TV and I won't hum their songs or ride in their cars or read their columns or watch them play ball. (I forgot to mention Roberto Clemente.) That way, no matter how great they are, I won't get blamed if they come to an early end.

Who am I kidding? We all NEED to have heroes. They point us in the right directions and give us strength. The problem is one of supply and demand. The demand is always there. The supply is not. Too bad ... for all of us.

A Treasure from my Son

I HAVE FOUR SONS. Each of them is unique and a source of pride and the object of my unconditional love. The youngest of them, Layne, was 9 weeks old when we adopted him in Mexico. That occurred more than 30 years ago.

It will not offend his brothers when I admit that there is a special bond between Layne and me. I will never understand how fate aligned the stars to bring us together with such intensity. It just happened.

Some time ago, I replaced my laptop computer and gave the discarded one to Layne. Several days later, though, I was required to retrieve a lost electronic file from the old computer. As I searched for the missing material, I came upon the following poem Layne had written.

When my eyes dried enough to do so, I sent it to my own e-mail address. Layne is not aware that I know this composition exists. It is something I will treasure for the rest of my life.

"Daddy"
(by Layne V. Miller)

Daddy…
My precious, daddy,
Tell me what can I do?
For so long you've been so strong.
But now life's caught up with you.

You're no longer the man,
Who can do all the things,
You could a few years ago.
And to make things worse,
This dreadful curse,
Is no fault of your own.

Life's not fair it's fair to say,
No point in trying to understand.
Bad things happen to good people,
All we can do is do what we can.
So we'll take each day as it comes,
And face it together me and you.
So daddy, my precious, daddy,
Tell me what can I do?
Cause, daddy, my precious, daddy,
Your boy loves you.

Happy…try to be happy.
In this one chance we have.
Try to smile if just for a while,
Take your mind off the bad.

Let us do what we like,
For as long as we can,
Try our best not to get down.
Let's make the most of this,
Beautiful gift of living while we're still around.

Life's not fair it's fair to say,
No point in trying to understand.
Bad things happen to good people,
All we can do is do what we can.
So we'll take each day as it comes,
And face it together me and you.
So daddy, my precious, daddy,
Tell me what can I do?
Cause, daddy, my precious, daddy,
Your boy loves you.

Some tears will be shed along the way,
When days get hard to make it through.
But together we'll face those bumpy roads.
Like a father and son should do.

So daddy, my precious, daddy,
Tell me how can I help you?
Cause, daddy, my precious, daddy,
Your boy loves you.

"I am strongly in favor of common sense, common honesty and common decency.
This makes me forever ineligible for public office."
H.L. Mencken, Columnist, *The Baltimore Sun*

What Has Happened To Us?

SOMEONE A LOT WISER than me once wrote: "Go quietly amid the noise and haste, and remember what peace there may be in silence." In keeping with that advice, my general rule is that I keep my serious thoughts to myself. But it's my rule, so I can break it if something really concerns me. And something does. It is about us – the American people. We have changed, and not in a good way.

A selfish, intolerant and hateful meanness has taken strong root in the spirit of many of our people. It has sprouted, grown and spread among us like a noxious weed since about 1990. I am worried and sad and ashamed and perplexed that we have come to this, and I fear that we may never, ever regain the high ground of compassion and diversity of our past.

True enough, we have never been perfect. Far from it. We've had our advocates of Jim Crow and Joe McCarthy and ethnic and religious intolerance. But on balance, we were an example to the world of an open, sensitive, forward-looking and caring people. Warts and all, ours was the world's benchmark society at the conclusion of World War II.

Look where we are now. We've abandoned most everything positive in our national character. We respond so predictably to negative, false and defamatory political ads that almost no candidate for public office can win without them. Qualifications don't count anymore. Many votes are cast based on which candidate has the meanest TV spot or the shortest list of semi-criminal baggage.

We applaud the closing of our borders to outsiders because we're afraid they'll take our jobs and fill our welfare roles. Based on our current attitudes, we should probably send the Statue of Liberty back to France.

Our government is in debt, so we blame the social safety nets our parents' generation established for the poor and disabled instead of the true causes. In fact, we abhor taxes, allow our mega corporations to avoid paying their share. We expect our government to protect us and respond to crises, but we don't want to pay for it. In fact, we all spent the money, and now we don't want to pay it back. We have no one to blame but ourselves.

Stress and financial over-extension is pervasive. It is a pox we have invited in. We purchase big and expensive things for personal fulfillment, but they cause more anxiety than pleasure. Our jobs dominate and define us. Family and friends and inner peace come last.

Our children pay the price. They spend their days even before they can walk in day care centers. When they're a little older, they come home to empty houses where supervision and a parent's touch are only dreams.

School is out for too many teens who have no parental governors. Guns, knives, drugs and defiance are everywhere in our schools.

From the largest corporation to the weakest milquetoast citizen, we all suffer the consequences. But the children – God help them – are the real victims of our desperate quest for more money, more things, more time for ourselves. What are they to do except to scream out in resentment and rebellion? What have we done?

We lock our doors in fear, both day and night. We trust no one we don't know and very few people we do know. We tell our children never to talk to strangers. And so every stranger is someone our tender youngsters need to fear. We tell them so.

I grew up in the 1950s. In those days, my parents would vote for the "best man for the job." And there usually was one. I can remember the German accents of immigrant relatives and the stories of how my Grandpa made a new life in this country by working hard, gaining for himself the respect of those who were here before him. I can remember my teachers telling me that this country was the "Great Melting Pot" with unlimited opportunity for those who would work hard and contribute. And it seemed like everyone did work hard. Everyone who could. And nobody talked bad about those who couldn't.

I can remember that policemen were respected because they were good, honest people who deserved our trust. Even though most of them still meet that standard, more than a few do not. Observe the result. They all suffer, and so do we. I can remember that doctors and lawyers were almost universally thought of as honorable people, and were relied upon in times of trouble. Now, if people seek their help, it is only with resentment and mistrust.

I can remember when everybody in the neighborhood knew everybody else and took care of one another's children and helped out in times of trouble. Now we complain when some kid we don't recognize walks through our back yard. Then, the next day, we find out he lives three doors down the street. And the only dog we know on sight is our own, the one we bought for protection. What have we done?

I can remember when my mother greeted the mailman and the milkman every day without worrying that someone would start an ugly rumor about her. I can remember when she answered the door unafraid of the stranger asking for odd jobs or a free meal or directions. Now we have peepholes in our doors and guns in our drawers and "stand-your-ground" laws. Strangers, especially those with different skin, are not welcome on our property. We send them away unkindly and quickly. And we shun them in public places. There is no effort to befriend them. It is too risky. Oh, the things we could learn if we would only open our minds. But we do not.

I can remember never coming home to an empty house because my mom was always there and my dad would soon follow. Dinner was cooked at home and was served at 5:30 every night and everybody had better be on time and washed up. We talked and laughed a lot at dinner. It was a time to be together, to be a family. I can remember that there were rules children had to follow and there was discipline when they didn't and the discipline worked and the kids grew up without psychological damage from it.

I can remember music, real music, on the radio. Music that did not suggest killing or total social irresponsibility. I can remember when Little League Baseball was fun for the kids who played it.

I can remember feeling safe at school and never seeing anyone with a weapon or drugs there. I can remember that everyone knew we should help the rest of the world just because it was the right thing to do – it was called "foreign aid." I can remember when we all wanted to get to the moon first and were willing to pay the price without complaining. I can remember when political leaders were leaders who could disagree without being disrespectful.

I can remember living in a country of ambition and hope and trust where kids loved their parents and pretty much did what they said, and where parents paid more attention to their children than to their own public images and where peace among neighbors and co-workers was the rule, not the exception. I can remember that people were not always late or in a hurry or overworked or afraid or crippled with stress. I can remember that people smiled a lot more and frowned a lot less and that kids had more fun and less to fear. What have we done? What have we done?

It was a time when selfish and mean-spirited ideas did not dominate our approach to one another, to government and to the world. It was a time when our fears were mostly in check, our prerogatives were mostly in order and our kids were pretty much okay. It wasn't that long ago. I don't know what we have done. But I know this: Sometimes I don't like us very much anymore.

College Bound

A FEW DAYS AGO, I overheard two women and a man in conversation at the next table during lunch. I've heard this same discussion among others many times before. It always saddens and puzzles me.

Lady #1 says that her youngest child will go off to college soon. She is so happy that her days of child-raising are almost over. She can hardly wait for her daughter to get packed up and take off. "Free at last," she says with a smile.

The man at the table is ahead of Lady #1. His kids have been gone a few years already. "It's been great," he says. "Kids are such a hassle, especially when they're young." All that chauffeuring them around and homework and teacher conferences and music lessons and sports. It seemed like it would never end, but it has. He says it's great to have that part of his life behind him. Soon (and he laughs) it'll be their turn to care of him. Is that funny, or what?

Lady #2 is younger. She still has two in grade school and one in diapers. She wishes aloud that she could be Lady #1. She feels trapped. Her kids drive her nuts. They're so much work – even more so on the weekends.

"Thank God for day care," she says. Her husband feels the same way. And all those private lessons and ball games and practices. They're just too much. Next year, she says, she won't let the older ones play little league. It ruins the summer nights and weekends for everyone else.

The man agrees. If he had it to do over, his boys wouldn't play baseball or soccer either. In fact, if the second kid had been first, there never would've been a second. That second kid was involved in every sport. After a few years of it, he told that boy he couldn't sign up any more; but he did anyway. So then he told him to find his own way to get there and back. That made things a lot simpler. And he did. "If they want to do that stuff," he told Lady #2, "make 'em do it on their own." His pride in his approach to parenting ruined my lunch. He didn't realize how lucky he was to have his kid on the practice field instead of in the poppy field.

And so it goes. It is one of the curses of our generation that these people, and so many like them, fill up their houses with kids, and then regard them as burdens to be endured rather than miracles to be treasured. I can only wonder why such people chose to have children in the first place. Especially a second or third child. If they didn't welcome the burden of one, why do it again? And why do it to the kids?

A negative approach to parenting is not lost on children. It brands their spirit and self-esteem. Hear me! Kids know when their parents wish they were childless. And hear me again. Limiting your kid's participation in activities or sports because it's too much hassle for mom and dad is a selfish mistake that you will pay for in spades. There is probably no better place for a child to benefit, both physically and socially, than an organized activity that challenges that child. And when a child is deprived of that kind of opportunity, he or she will likely find other, less wholesome, ways to expend the same energy.

Parenting is a 24 hour per day job and it's not for everybody. So people should not have a child just because everybody else does. Usually, we have the choice of conceiving a child or not. It is a choice that will affect at least three lives forever. Not a choice to be made lightly or on a whim.

Nevertheless, many among us have two, three or more children, but declare to the world a wish that they had none. It's understandable, perhaps, that parents might bring one child into the world, not knowing they don't have what it takes to do it right. But if a person doesn't like being the parent of one child, it's a pretty good bet another one isn't gonna make things better.

True parenting means to be involved in your children's lives constantly from birth to emancipation. That is the only way to do it right. And every child's needs will be different.

In the early years, they're helpless without you. They depend on you to feed and clothe them, to bathe and hold them, to teach them to speak and walk and love and obey and to smile. In the middle years, you are coach, teacher, companion, advisor, disciplinarian, provider, transporter, spectator and more. In the years just before college, you'll be in their way – which is exactly where you need to be – ever watchful of their friends and activities. They may have very little to say to you during that time, either because they'll be busy trying to figure out how to get you out of their way or because they think they don't need you much anymore. But they do. Make them talk and make them listen. They'll be glad when you do.

Until the late high school years, every kid should be kept involved in every organized sport, activity, arts program and summer sports camp a parent can find and afford. Just sign 'em up, pay the fees, and figure out a way to get 'em there, whether they want to go or not. Because when a kid is on an athletic field, or in a piano lesson, or learning to debate, that kid can't be somewhere else getting into trouble with kids who are idle. Keep them involved, and stay involved with them, to the point of exhaustion. Yours and theirs.

Just as they should make it to every practice, you've got to be there every time they compete or perform. And you should clap and yell and wave and make sure they know you're there and that you're watching.

Very few kids who feel important and exhausted ever cause trouble. And very few parents who interact with their kids in that way will be happy to see them grow up and leave.

A few days ago, one of the two young ones I have still at home turned eighteen. It was a melancholy day for me, because I know that next year, he'll be away from us in college and pretty much on his own. As he drove off to school that day, I remembered that each time one of his older siblings left for college it was a sad day in my life. A day that changed the order of things in a dramatic way. A day that left a silence in my house that I will miss forever.

He and his little sister are sleeping right now. They're worn out. So am I and so is their mom. But I'm not tired of having them around. And you'll never hear me tell anyone how happy I'll be when they're gone.

A Question of Leadership

IN 1960, with the Cold War at its hottest, I. I. Rabi, an immigrant American physicist who had won the Nobel Prize for his work on the Manhattan Project, wrote in the Atlantic Monthly about America's image and role in the world. Remember, this was almost 50 years ago:

"Those of us who travel abroad and have the problem of representing the United States in one way or another are often taken aback at the degree and intensity of criticism that is directed both at our actions and at the statements of some of our political figures. No such intense criticism is directed at the Soviet Union for acts compared with which our own slips would seem to be minor. At first sight, the criticism which holds us to a stricter accounting seems unfair. However, if one probes more deeply, this attitude is quite natural.

"We must understand," he continued, "that we occupy an entirely different position in the world from that of the Russians. Not only is the United States the leader of the Western world, but to an extent greater than we realize, the United States is the leader of the whole world. Beneath the scoffing, mocking, and hostility of the Communist world, there is nevertheless a deep respect. America is the ideal, not only materially but in most elements of existence which human beings share in common. If America were to disappear, there would be no embodiment of the Russian goal, no one to catch up with and surpass. For these reasons, when we fall short of the high standards which we and the world have set for us, the failure is felt very deeply. The elevated and rarefied moral atmosphere in which we are supposed to live may be a bit hard on us plain folks here at home, but it is the role which we have assumed and the role which we have to play.

"If one can be certain of anything in the uncertain course of events...it is this: the moment the United States stops supplying leadership, the world as we know it will disintegrate and fragment into chaos..."

Much has transpired since those words were written. We have been to the brink of atomic destruction with a president who was later murdered. We have weathered civil unrest born of racial strife and the national gut-wrenching that was Vietnam.

We have seen presidents fall from grace to shame. We have agonized over hostages in Iran and peacekeepers killed by terrorists. We have sent our treasure and our youth to every corner of this earth to help others, sometimes armed to the teeth, sometimes as the Peace Corps. We have brokered peace in some places and imposed it in others. We patiently turned the screws and watched as the communist experiment crumbled without a shot being fired. The Soviet Union is gone–vanished. And now, we are under attack by hate-filled Islamic extremists who call us devils.

All of that has happened since Mr. Rabi wrote about the need for prudent and patient American leadership. But our predominant position on the world stage has not changed.

We are not devils. We know that. But at one time or another, almost every other nation and every religious sect on this planet has resented our actions, our inaction or our success. Then, at other times, most of those same people have looked to us for help. And we have given it.

Try for a moment to imagine what this world would be like if we had not done some of the courageous and noble things we have done. Imagine if JFK had blinked first in 1961. Imagine if Martin Luther King's message had not been one of peace. Imagine if we had closed our borders to the Cubans, Haitians, Mexicans, Vietnamese, Africans, Indians and all those who now are part of us. Imagine the world with unchallenged ayatollahs, unchecked Stalins, unafraid Saddams.

It is neither surprising nor embarrassing that our leadership decisions and policies have often been driven by what our government perceived to be in America's own best interests. That, after all, is the government's job. But, in our pride, we need to recognize that we aren't perfect.

We have, when it suited us, pursued friendships with evil, unworthy and repressive governments. We turned a blind eye to the suffering they created, and by our silence condoned their disregard for basic human rights. We have tolerated corruption when it advanced our cause and condemned corruption when it did not. We have been the honest broker of peace between warring factions; and at other times we've been less than even-handed. There is a price to be paid for that kind of duplicity. More so for us, as Dr. Rabi said in 1960, because we are the nation the whole world at once envies, emulates, loves, hates and depends upon.

As we pursue the current just cause against the evils of terrorism, we are sometimes shocked and outraged when we hear that many people on every continent are critical of us, even angered, by our aggressive response to the events of September 11. What they see, and the only thing they see, is the arrogance that accompanies unmatched military power. What many of them think is that because of our arrogance and insensitivity, we had September 11 coming.

And we wonder: How can that possibly be? We are the good guys. We didn't ask for this fight. We were attacked. So we will again take the lead. We will protect ourselves first, and we will again pay the bill. We will again help rebuild not one, but two, vanquished nations. Just as we did 60 years ago.

So why, we wonder--why are so many so angry with us? And why are they not all with us? Much of the world, not only the Arabs, shouts the answer. But most of us, and our leaders, dismiss it. We should not. Because when we do, we compromise our own safety and even more significantly our ability to lead. Listen to them:

"Yes," they say, "We, too, condemn the attacks of September 11, but we do not trust you. We respect your right to defend your homeland, but what of your treatment of us? Your words of high honor and purpose do not match your policies and your actions. Terror is not a new problem. It is only new to you. Because, until now, you have ignored our agonies at the hands of violent fanatics. And neither are hunger and disease new. They have been our daily companions. Where have you been, America? Where have you been with your wealth and comfort and security, while we have starved and struggled and died? Where have you been?

"Where were your planes and guns and soldiers when we were being tortured and slaughtered? They were not in Afghanistan or in Iraq, until you felt threatened. They were not in Chile or Columbia. They were not in Africa where millions were slaughtered. They were not in Kashmir or in East Timor. They did not depose a hundred tyrants whose friendship you courted for oil or military bases or for leverage against the Soviet threat. You may be the mightiest nation, but you are not our leader because you have not been fair and even-handed.

"And where were your miracle AIDS drugs and doctors when our babies were dying? Where were you? They are dying still. Where are you?

"You are self-serving, deceptive and duplicitous. We do not trust you. And because we do not trust you, we will not follow."

That is what most of the world says to us. And most of the world is, mostly, right.

The global leadership responsibility of this great nation has only increased since 1960. But our image is badly tarnished by our performance. We have shared our wealth, but too little. We have helped our neighbors, but only when it suited us. We have defended human rights more than most, but not always.

The game is more complex, and the names and motives of our enemies are different, but the basic unmet needs of most of the world's people are the same as they were in 1960. And the cup will not pass from us. There wasn't anyone there to take it from us in 1960, and there's no one there to take it from us now. The difference is that we've made the task of exercising leadership a good deal more difficult because, despite our good intentions, and despite our belief that we are the kindest, most generous people on earth, we've been selfish, isolated, and arrogant too often. We are making the same mistakes that every other superpower in history has made. And those mistakes will bring us down just as surely.

It is true that in modern history, no other nation than ours has been so willing to support a world order of peace among nations and peoples. But too often, we view an international problem as a matter of "us or them". We fail to address the causes of the unrest that, in turn, creates our own insecurity. Too often, we either attack, threaten to attack or leave a desperate people to their own devices, when none of those are the best solution. They are mistakes so basic and insensitive that we shouldn't be surprised when even our friends doubt our good intentions.

At every level of human interaction, from the family to the international community, there is an achievable balance between appeasement and force, between self-interest and compassion, between intransigence and negotiation. It is a leader's obligation to pursue that balance every day and in every matter. We are the leader, but we haven't always done that.

We don't mean to be, but we are too often arrogant. We are too prosperous and too powerful to act unilaterally, brushing aside the legitimate concerns of allies and others of goodwill. We should never support corrupt leaders when they should be left to the mercy of their own people. We should not, indeed we cannot, ignore the desperate when we have the resources and technology or science to help them. The Aids epidemic is only the most pressing example of our failure in this regard.

We have professed a consistent resolve to correct the wrongs of this world without a desire for territorial dominance. In that way, we are unique. But we are not perfect. And we should stop allowing our leaders to assert that we are.

What Dr. Rabi recognized in 1960 is still true. We're the only game in town right now. And we're the only ones who can screw it up. If we don't find the right balance, if we continue to turn inward, if our approach to solving the world's injustices is not measured and fair, our preeminence will not last very long because it will only be based upon our muscles.

We are the only leader now, mostly because we have the most muscles. Those who exercised leadership in the past based only upon muscles have been miserable failures. Muscle is required, no doubt. But leadership requires more. It requires wisdom, restraint, humility and charity as much as it requires muscle. We've got to get it right. If we don't, what is your guess for who will replace us? And how do you think we'll like it when somebody else is calling the shots?

Times Have Changed

TIMES HAVE CHANGED. When I was ten years old, if my teacher (pronounced "Nun") had phoned my parents with the message that I had not turned in my homework for an entire week, no discussion would have ensued and no explanations would have been accepted. The scene, which never occurred because I wanted to live to be eleven, would have unfolded something like this:

My Dad:	"David, come down here." (the word "please" was not used with children.)
David:	"Yes sir?"
My Dad:	"Sister Cunnegunda (I could not make up that name) called your mother today about your homework. She says she thinks you're lazy. She says you haven't turned any homework assignments in for a week. It that true?"
David:	"Yes sir."
My Dad:	"Bend over, son." (Please note that my Dad would have no interest in determining why I had not done my homework; and that justice was swift in my house.)

Now today, if I received such a phone call from my daughter's teacher, Mrs. Swaggle, here is a slightly abridged version (ignoring the pleasantries) of how I believe that conversation would go:

Mrs. Swaggle:	"Hello Mr. Miller. I'm sorry to bother you but I'm concerned because Sage hasn't been turning in her homework lately."
Me as Dad:	"Oh, really?"
Mrs. Swaggle:	"Yes sir. I do hope this isn't a reflection of her feelings toward me. I've been worried about that for several days. I've noticed that she seems to have some issues with me. I just don't know what to do. It's been about a two weeks since she's turned in any homework.
Me as Dad:	"Oh, really, two weeks; and you're just calling now?"
Mrs. Swaggle:	"Yes sir. I didn't want to seem unreasonable. Do you think you might be able to talk to Sage about this? I'm very concerned about her grades, you know, if she doesn't do the necessary work."

Me as Dad:	"Yes, I will. Don't worry about it anymore Mrs Swaggle. I'll take care of it."
Mrs. Swaggle:	"Oh, thank you, Mr. Miller. I just knew you would talk to her."

And so I would assume my most authoritative posture and I would speak with Sage about this matter. Here, I suspect, would be the substance of our conversation:

Me as Dad:	"Sage, come down here."
Mother:	"Now David, don't be too harsh. You didn't even say please."
Sage:	"What do you want? I'm on line."
Me as Dad:	"I don't care if you're on line. Come down here, right now."
Sage:	"Okay, but you don't have to be rude about it. You didn't even say please."
Me as Dad:	"That's because it isn't a request, it's a command. Come here."
Mother:	"Now David, settle down. She's been so sweet lately."
Sage:	"Okay, I'm here. What do you want? And anyway, what's a command?"

Me as Dad:	"I want to know why you haven't done your homework for the last two weeks." (This would be my first mistake--asking "why." There is no acceptable excuse short of hospitalization. But notice that I would bravely ignore the "command" issue.)
Sage:	"Oh, that. The homework thing. (Her face curls in exasperation.) How did you find out?"
Me as Dad:	"Mrs. Swaggle called me; that's how."
Sage:	"She is such a Drip. I know the stuff. I can pass the tests. I just decided that if I did all the homework she assigns, I'd never have any social life. I told mom that. She understands, but I knew you wouldn't.
Me as Dad:	"Sage, there is nothing to understand. You are 10. You don't have a social life. And even if you did, schoolwork takes priority. You must do that first. No exceptions. If you don't do your school work, I'll

	guarantee you that you won't have a social life – not any – at all."
Sage:	(Looking at her Mom) "Can he do that? I have rights you know!"
Mother:	"Now, Sage, be careful, your Dad's already pretty upset."
Me as Dad:	"I am not upset. I am mad. Sage, you are grounded until all of the homework you haven't done is completed; and I want to see it before you turn it in."
Sage:	"Okay. That means I have until Friday to do it all."
Me as Dad:	"Why is that? Why do you have 'til Friday?"
Sage:	"Because I don't have any plans until then. G'Night, daddy."

My own dad is gone now. I wish I could call him on the phone tonight. I feel like I need another lesson in Childhood Discipline 101. Because I knew from the start that somewhere in that conversation, if it ever occurs, I will lose the momentum. Maybe because times have changed for the worse. I don't tell my kids to "Bend over." Maybe because I'm pretty sure that if I did, Sage wouldn't. No, not "maybe." I'm sure.

Mama always said, 'Life was like a box of chocolates. You never know what you're gonna get.' – Forrest Gump, the Motion Picture

Prologue to a Matter of Bad Timing

THE AUTHOR'S DAD, Vincent A. Miller, was born in 1917 on the west side of Evansville, Indiana, and grew to adulthood there. His family lost their home to foreclosure during the Great Depression. Vincent attended Memorial High School, located on the far eastern edge of the city. There he met his future wife, Augusta Greif, and graduated in 1934, when he was barely 18. His family did not have an automobile, nor the money to pay streetcar fare to and from the high school, so Vincent used his clip-on roller skates to travel the five-mile route each school day, rain or shine. For financial reasons, college was out of the question; but Vincent never gave up that dream.

Immediately after high school graduation, he went to work in a factory and attended die-making classes at a local trade school. Although he contracted a nearly fatal kidney infection in 1936 that confined him to bed for six months, by the age of 21, he was a master die-maker at Servel, Inc.

When the U.S. entered World War II, his skill and reputation as a precision die-maker was so well known that he was placed in charge of a team of much older and more experienced men. Vincent's team developed and maintained the very precise tooling required for the production of the wing assemblies used on U.S fighter planes that were locally assembled.

After the war, Servel moved Vincent into new job responsibilities as its "last resort" troubleshooter, which involved long hours and extensive travel. Still, during this period in the late 1940s and 1950s, Vincent developed numerous skills that he used to earn extra money for his family. He sold custom-made dress suits; he made hand-braided wool rugs and refinished antique furniture. College became a dream that was blowing in the wind because of the fast pace of his life. But he finally caught up with that dream when he retired in 1986.

Eight years of classes, intertwined with numerous speaking engagements and the publication of several successful instructional books, finally brought him to graduation day at Western Michigan University in Kalamazoo, Michigan. I told him throughout those eight years that he needed that college degree about as much as he needed another hole in his head. He responded each time, in a very soft voice, that I would never understand. And he told me again and again in a very quiet but resolute tone that he was going to get his college degree for numerous reasons that were personal to him and he did not intend to discuss those reasons with me or with anybody else. And he never did. He just kept whatever promise he had made to himself and clearly enjoyed every minute of his university education.

The article below was my tribute to the pride and determination that drove my dad to achieve that ultimate dream – an achievement that the timing and circumstances of his birth, childhood and family responsibilities would have denied to a lesser man.

A Matter of Bad Timing

The Evansville Courier
Friday, June 23, 1995

There is this kid who grew up in the 1920s on Evansville's west side. Big kid, smart kid. Strong and fast and a fearless kid to a sensible point. It wasn't his fault, but in those early years the timing always seemed to be wrong. When he was 12, the market crashed and the depression set in. His dad lost the house. He was a year ahead of his contemporaries in school. His mom put him in first grade one year early. He was smart enough alright, but he was always a half-step slower and a few inches shorter than his classmates, because they were older. It wasn't such a big deal until high school when he was cut from the basketball team to make space for an underclassman who showed promise. He should have been that underclassman, but his timing was off.

The mid 1930s were a bad time to graduate from high school if you were a boy, especially if you were a boy from a family who had lost about everything in the depression. That's when this west side kid graduated – bad timing. There was a war brewing in Europe, and both jobs and money were scarce. His dad couldn't send him to college, nor did he care to try. The family was financially down and out. The kid wanted to go to college real bad, but the time was not right. On top of that, he got sick – very sick. His kidneys almost shut down. He almost shut down. The kid never forgot about the college diploma he didn't have. But when he got well, he had to go back to work.

The war brought jobs and long work days at the plant. He married his high school girlfriend. Those were busy years. The war, taking care of his wife's father, a baby boy, second jobs and odd jobs to make ends meet, but always some precious time with those he loved – not enough, but some. More kids, more work – traveling now thousands and thousands of miles every year on the job. So little time for himself, none in fact. When the kid from the west side wasn't working, he was working. He sold custom-made suits, he refinished furniture, he made braided wool rugs. He was a photographer, mechanic, family repairman, inventor and, oh yeah, a dad. That took time too.

In his twenties and thirties at Servel and then Whirlpool, he demonstrated over and over again a unique ability to fix what no one else could fix and to teach others how he had solved unsolvable problems. However, when he reached management level, he still didn't have that college degree. He knew more, reasoned better and accomplished more than those MBAs he answered to, but he didn't have his ticket to the inner circle. So they admired him and praised him and liked him very much.

They kept him very busy and they kept him on the outer edge of the corporate leadership.

It is ironic that his job was to teach. More ironic yet, he became the teacher of teachers, the leader of those in American industry whose jobs were to teach others how to do their jobs. He was the Dean of Industrial Teachers, but the west side kid didn't have the piece of paper the MBAs had. So they never opened the door.

There was never any question as I and my siblings grew up that we would go to college, that we would graduate, that when the time came, the right doors would open. That was all because we were the kids of the kid from the west side, and he made certain as we grew that we would have those advantages – at his expense.

One of my favorite characters in literature is the scarecrow in the Wizard of Oz. He was decent and loyal. His priorities were perfect. His logic was always right. It was he who led the group to safety. But he wanted a "brain." So when he finally got to the Wizard, the Wizard gave him a diploma. For if you have a diploma, the Wizard reasoned, you must have a brain. And the scarecrow had already demonstrated that he had a wonderful, fertile brain.

So it is with the kid from the West Side of Evansville. He has traveled down a yellow brick road 60 years since he graduated from Memorial High School. At every turn and every bump, he has solved every problem with his intelligence, his resourcefulness, his knowledge of both technical and social matters. In the meantime, he raised and educated four children. And now, after he has seen to the needs of everyone else, he has found the time to jump through the Wizard's hoops so he can have his diploma. He has even mastered computers and published three books in the process.

Like the scarecrow, the kid from the west side only had to get that diploma for himself. Everyone else knew a long time ago how special and gifted he is. But his diploma serves a great purpose, nonetheless. It fills a void in the heart of a man who always put everyone else's needs above his own and whose personal achievements could be the envy of most of his generation. I knew he was smart from the day I met him. I didn't need a diploma to convince me, and I don't need one now.

But now he'll have it, and I'm so proud of him I could bust. My dad, Vincent A. Miller, Memorial High School Class of 1934, will graduate from Western Michigan University in Kalamazoo on June 24, 1995. He was 78 in February. He has almost a straight A average. Under ordinary circumstances, he could probably land a pretty good job. Eventually he would make some company a great CEO.

The only thing wrong is the timing.

Dad's Book

Evansville Courier & Press
Thursday, February 4, 1999

A NEW BOOK was published on Christmas Day, 1998, about growing up on Evansville's west side and about 82 years of family life in the semi-fast lane of the 20th century. My dad wrote it.

It's a simple book, in simple prose, about a real life. His life. It isn't for sale. There are only five copies. That's all there ever will be. One for him, and one for each of his kids.

For him, it was a labor of love. For me, it's a gift I'll always treasure. Because, in addition to its stories and wisdom, this small book sends an unspoken message its author never intended--a message larger than the book itself.

The message is that we all have within us memories and feelings that make us each unique. But they're rarely discussed. I didn't know much about my dad's childhood or what had shaped his drive and resolve until he wrote this book. Now, I can see right into his being. I can see that he is both complex and uncomplicated, like the Franklin hill neighborhood where he grew up when there was a president named Coolidge and later during the hardest of times. I understand how vulnerability and strength can develop side by side.

Until now, his early days seemed like simpler times. Now I know the pain he must have felt when his parents lost their home. That kind of experience has a way of shaping lives and building quiet resolve. Until now, the history books I've read were about world events on a grand scale. This book contains a more relevant variety of history, explaining events I watched unfold and speaking to my own roots.

Most of us want to feel that we've left this place a little better than we found it. And most of us want those we care about to know who we've been and what we've accomplished. Our children need that information so they can better understand us and measure themselves against us. And because they love us. Remember, no matter your age or theirs, a parent never stops being a parent.

Anyway, I'm not sure there needs to be a reason. The fact is, if we don't preserve our personal stories, thoughts and feelings, they will die with us. If that's what you want to happen, there is no sin in it. But I believe each of us has some experience and gains some wisdom in this life that nobody else ever had before. When we write those things down, we give something back to this planet that nurtured and supported us, and to our children who want to know what it was like, and what we did and what we thought and felt, when the world was young.

Oh, I almost forgot. Thanks, Dad.

An Anniversary for Some Role Models

The Evansville Press
Friday, October 11, 1996

O**N SEPTEMBER 14, 1940, my parents were married at St. Anthony's Church on First Avenue. It was a perfect September day. I've seen pictures of them at the outdoor reception. They were dancing. In 1996, I forgot to call them on their 56th anniversary. When I remembered, late in the evening, I didn't think it mattered too much that I had forgotten. They probably wouldn't have been home to take my call earlier in the day anyway. They would have been at the Notre Dame-Purdue football game. And I was right; they were.

It was almost 10:30 at night. I could have called right then to say, "Happy Anniversary." But I didn't. I said to myself, "What's the use? They don't need to hear from me this late. It's their anniversary. They're celebrating." And I learned later that I was right about that too. When I went to bed they were, indeed, celebrating. The Lord knows, and so do I, that there aren't many people who, at age 53, can call two healthy parents on the telephone and wish them a happy anything. I was lucky in that respect. But the way these two people behaved made it difficult for me to make a big deal about how lucky I was.

Not only did I not think of them as old, THEY didn't think of themselves that way. I mean, my dad had just graduated from college. He had started graduate school a couple of weeks ago. My mom still got speeding tickets and griped about the cops. It was like having parents who never grew up.

So finally, a day late, I called. Mom answered. She always answered during non-business hours. During business hours, dad answered from his office upstairs. (Yes, his office.) He worked there every day at his computer. Mom told me all about the football game. It was raining, but no matter – they had their rain gear – they were fine. They had been season-ticket-holders at Notre Dame since the middle sixties. That's my sister's fault. Her college roommate was the daughter of Ara's secretary and the rest is history.

So during the last thirty years, my parents had been to maybe two hundred Notre Dame Football games. All the others they've watched on TV. My mother won't allow anyone in the family to cheer for a Notre Dame opponent. I graduated from the University of Michigan. A long time ago. I don't rely upon my parents for financial support, and I had six kids of my own. None of this, however, qualified me to root for UM against God's team. It was serious business with her.

I heard about the two pre-game parties they went to and how many of their grandchildren they saw at the game. I learned they had four free tickets from Mom's cousin so they took my sister, one of my brothers and their spouses along. One of my own adult sons was there, found them in the crowd, and spent some time. All in all, a busy day.

After the game, they drove the 40 miles back to their home in St. Joe, Michigan. They had to hurry so they'd be there in time to go to dinner with all their children, except me. They had a great time at dinner, but she complained that my sister and brothers had all gone home by 10:30. "I guess they were tired," she said in a complaining tone of voice. I did not mention that 10:30 was about the time I went to bed too.

So there they were, just she and dad, alone in their house at 10:30 on their 56th wedding anniversary. At first she didn't like it at all that they were all alone. "What's wrong with these young kids, anyway?" she thought. "Why do they go home so early? Especially on a night like this!" That's what she was thinking.

So she and my dad decided to turn on their CD player. Because, unlike their pansy children, they were not tired. And do you know what they did then? They danced. They danced together, and they kept dancing until one o'clock in the morning, right there in their own parlor. Their big old Victorian house had large windows. Passersby can see right in when the lights are on. But they didn't care. They danced, as they had danced on their wedding day and all the anniversaries since then. And as they have since their wedding and on the 55 anniversaries before this one, when they were finished dancing, they went to bed – together.

We had a nice conversation. I didn't get fussed at a bit for not calling the day before. They didn't care; they were too busy to take my call anyway.

We hear a lot these days about the need for parental role models. I think some aging baby boomers need role models worse than some of their own youngsters. They are gone now, but I would have put those two up against all comers. They didn't intend it, but they were a living model for other married people. They spoke with their lives and here is their lesson: As long as you're alive, and whether you have a partner or not, fill up every day with life. And when you're 79 years old, or when you're 179 years old, if you like to dance, and if you can dance, then turn the music on, take someone you like by the hand, and dance. Whatever you want to do, and if you can do it; do it. Always, every day, keep your brain and your body busy and challenged and at work. Because if you don't, no matter how old you are, or how old you aren't, you'll probably have to go home early. And you'll miss the dance.

Moderation

ONE SPRING DAY in 1960, a young history teacher walked into his classroom at Memorial High School and wrote on the blackboard: "MODERATION IN ALL THINGS."

For the next forty minutes, without notes or textbook for reference, young Brother James Sullivan spoke wisdom beyond his years. It was unlike any other high school class I remember. Thirty teenage boys quietly listened. And the simple lesson he taught that day reverberates now, maybe more than ever.

Brother James said that history is filled with periods when large masses of good people were influenced and dominated by fanatics. He said humans tend to be passive and non-confrontational. He said that most people, even in prosperous countries, focus their energies upon the well-being of their families, and thus leave to others the development of social and governmental policies. He said those "others" often are obsessed with narrow issues or a lust for power.

He said the tendency of good people to default in matters of policy leaves a vacuum that invites dominance by fanatics. He said it is difficult for moderates to match the passion of fanatics in any public debate.

Making matters worse, Brother James said, our generation was soft and complacent because we were pampered by parents who had lived through depression and war. He said our parents were stronger by ten than we would ever be, but their desire to assure our prosperity blinded them to the need to teach us to be tough and attentive to social and governmental issues and to be aggressive and vigilant against extremism.

He said that vigilance and attention to moderation were the best defenses against all extremes. He said our generation must be the next guardians and advocates of moderation and its by-products, tolerance and diversity. But he was not optimistic that we would accept the challenge.

"Moderation In All Things," he said, is the wellspring of wisdom. He said moderation in personal behavior and in government requires blending many ideas to create balance and avoid extremes. He said to beware of religion invading government and to resist rigid, intolerant concepts of governance or social behavior, no matter their source. He said the rule, "Moderation In All Things," should guide our every judgment and aspiration as adults.

This was heavy stuff for 16-year-olds. "Extremism" and "moderation" were not even in our lexicons. The world was simple. "Ike" was president. Elvis was singing. Everybody over thirty liked Ike. Everybody under thirty liked Elvis.

Brother James said that soon the debate would not be between Ike and Elvis. He said we were on a collision course with fanatics at both ends of the spectrum who would be blind to the harm of imposing their own social or governmental standards upon the rest of us. He said when that fury came, we should defend the high ground of moderation. But we have not.

Moderation, today, has few champions. It is dying from indifference. The battle for the high ground now is between the far right and the far left because we, in the center, allow fanatics to define the debate. Still, the wisdom of Brother James entreats us to devote our collective energy to the restoration of moderation.

Unless we do that together soon, we will deserve an "F," and all of its consequences.

Growing Old

Evansville Courier & Press
Wednesday, January 30, 2002

I'VE LATELY BEEN TENDING to some matters for a number of elderly people. These duties fall my way, by coincidence, when I'm beginning to come to grips with my own mortality. I have concluded in these circumstances that, in the main, growing old is a very unpleasant business.

Aging can rob us of our dignity. For the proud and formerly self-sufficient, that is the most dreaded impact of growing old. But it is an impact that the kindness, awareness and patience of others can cushion. The problem is that kindness, awareness and patience are often in short supply.

The surviving members of what Tom Brokaw labeled "The Greatest Generation" are now ours to care for, and more importantly, to care about. They are a proud and courageous lot. Between 1930 and 1945, they faced and defeated a combination of evils and tribulations that put our present troubles at the level of a skinned knee. If the few who remain have earned nothing else, they've earned our respect. Yet, too many times, we see them dishonored or pushed aside by those who owe them the greatest debt.

On a personal level, we've seen some of them treated with impatience and disdain by their own selfish children. To such ingrates, the elderly are inconvenient burdens, one more tax upon the younger person's time and energy. On a political level, it is part of the sport to make grand promises of more financial security and better medical benefits for the aged, grand promises that are never kept. The old folks know very well when they are the objects of such treatment by their children and their government. But what can they do about it? Usually, nothing. So it is for us who are not yet in the grip of old age, all of us, to create some space in our hearts, some time in our schedules and some political follow-up for those who are.

If you require a selfish motive to do that, think of it this way. We, the baby boomers, are the next generation of elders. So, we owe it to ourselves to raise the levels of empathy and compassion in this society for the aged and their issues, because our own old age is fast upon us.

My recent duties have brought to me another conclusion about growing old. I saw this same conclusion expressed on a bumper sticker last week. It said: "Growing old ain't for sissies."

Growing old is losing friends, siblings and mates and missing them the rest of your life.

Growing old is knowing that you'll never earn another dollar. What you have is all you will ever have and God help you if you live so long that it's all gone.

Growing old is doctors and hospitals and medicines and having to place so much trust in money-driven people and money-driven institutions who answer to money-driven HMO's and money-driven insurance companies when your health hangs in the balance.

Growing old is wanting not to be a burden on those you love and believing that you are nothing else but that to anybody.

Growing old is being alone, and lonely, a lot, and often. Empty time in silent, empty spaces where you long in vain for someone just to call or to knock. Someone just to visit with. And trying to remain composed and dignified when someone does.

Growing old is dealing with fear. Fear of evil people who prey on the helpless and near-helpless. Fear of a crippling fall. Fear of being alone when you really need help. Fear of more pain, more hospitals. And the worst fear, the fear of nursing homes where you are sure the most helpless of the old are sent and forgotten by everyone they love. Fear of fear.

Growing old is trying to sign your name, or drink a cup of coffee, or eat some soup, while the hand that served you so well for so many years tremors.

Growing old is hurting every time you walk, and requiring help to get into cars or to negotiate a few stairs or to rise from a chair.

Growing old is abandoning the premise that every day you are given should be lived to the fullest and believing instead that you are useless excess baggage, of no importance to anyone.

Growing old is walkers and canes and wheelchairs and struggling to accomplish the most basic human tasks, like getting dressed or bathing.

Growing old is the dread of creeping dementia.

Forget that "golden years" baloney. Growing old is tough duty. Seems to me it would be pretty hard to smile in such circumstances and even harder to keep any kind of positive attitude. But I know a great many elders who do. They take the hand they are dealt and make the very best of it. They might complain some. Who wouldn't? They might have some bad days. Who wouldn't? But mostly, they make their way through old age with a grace and pride that belies the challenges and worry they face every day. Because they ain't sissies. Growing old requires courage. Remember that when your own turn comes. And remember it too when it's your turn to help some of them.

Perfect Moment

JULY 4, 2014. Doing two of my favorite things at the same time – taking a peaceful morning walk and pushing a baby stroller occupied by my very content 10-month-old granddaughter.

I was singing softly to Vallie as we made our way slowly around the peaceful neighborhood where it is our good fortune to reside. She was my only audience and, although she could not yet talk, I sensed her approval by her expressive eyes, her smiles and her peaceful mood.

As we passed well-kept lawns and homes surrounding sparkling suburban lakes, we were absorbing the sights, the creatures and the fresh air of her new world. A pair of rabbits caught her eyes as they scurried from one protective bush to another, stopping in the midst of their dashes to make security checks. Birds and geese passed overhead. Creation was momentarily serene and quiet. Nary a person nor a moving vehicle intruded from any direction.

The day could not have been more perfect. A sky as blue and as clear as ever it gets in southern Indiana. A gentle breeze dancing around us. Low humidity and a temperature in the mid-70's. All in all, a blessed morning.

It occurred to me that Vallie was, in that moment, in the midst of an experience that was as close to simple, uncomplicated perfection as she was ever likely to have. I was wishing, as parents and grandparents have for all time, that I could protect this precious child forever from the inevitable blows of fate, and that all of her days could be like this one. My mind involuntarily reminded me of these lyrics from a song I have known for many years: "Dream away, child. Let your dreams run wild. For the years and the tears shed might claim you."

Moving ever so slowly around a bend, there appeared a panorama of nature, with a lake glittering in the sun populated by eight or ten baby geese and their mother and a wide expanse of trees, flowers and grass. Vallie sat up and looked straight ahead, taking it all in, and then turned her head to look at me. Her smile told me that, instinctively, she felt the love and natural power of the moment. I smiled back at her and, with her eyes fixed squarely upon mine, I said: "You're right, Little One. This is about as good as it gets."

There have only been a few times during my life when I have consciously begged time to stand still. This was one of them. It was a moment that, had it been possible, Vallie could hold onto, treasure, keep in reserve – a shield to call upon in years to come when her tears are falling or when events overtake her and serenity is elusive. But, alas, an infant's memory cannot preserve for later the wonder, security, inner peace and joy experienced as a small child. Vallie will never be able to recreate the mix of sensations, emotion and unconditional love that came together on that morning in July when life offered up a perfect moment.

So these words are for Vallie to read, especially when fate threatens to claim her precious smile. May they assure her that not only once upon a perfect day in July, but also on every other day, the world is hers and she is loved beyond measure. May they give her the comfort of knowing that her Papa's spirit will always be with her and will protect the serenity and security that are her birthright. And, most of all, may these words ever remind Vallie that each time she feels the gentle, dancing breeze kiss her cheek, it is just her Papa, keeping his promise.

Dog Walks

WHEN THE SUN is just rising, it is ever so quiet and peaceful on the nearby golf course. It is before the golfers and the double bogies of the day that my dog and I walk the cart paths. A few guys from the ground crew, smiling Hispanics mostly, keep the grass in check and soften the sand in the traps that will soon see their next guests. But for now – for these few early morning moments, it isn't a golf course at all. It is a place of respite where my dog and I become one with nature's trees and lakes, birds and squirrels, an occasional deer, the fresh air and the hills.

Like people everywhere, I encounter my daily share of challenges and I carry them wherever I go. They test our fortitude and weigh on our minds. But here, like another dimension, is a place where we can and must lay them down at the entrance. And in this dimension we can do nothing except experience creation and absorb its peace with the one other creature on this planet who loves us without condition. The mind can race out of control when it is set free in these conditions. It can explore previously buried crevices of thought and memory. Long-forgotten experiences can reappear in vivid detail. Tender moments, painful moments, proud moments and small successes from the past flash into view without warning. Then, without warning, we return to the present, with its sounds of chirping birds, a panting dog and the fresh morning breeze.

It is a trip to the same place every day that is different each time – a trip worth taking. And the dog loves it.

Bettye's Spirit

THIS STORY IS TRUE. I experienced every moment of it. How and why this sequence of events took place will remain a mystery to me for the rest of my life. If ever, the forces that were at work will only be revealed in another time and place.

My wife's mother, Bettye, passed away some years ago after a long illness. Bettye was a beautiful woman. She was a gentle, positive and loving wife and mother. Beyond all else, however, she was meticulous in every phase of her activities. Her house was spotlessly clean. There was never an unwashed plate in her kitchen or an out-of-place item in her bath. And she never, never received a visitor or ventured forth unless she was perfectly dressed and groomed.

When we were told by hospice that the end was near, I was asked to sort through a large box containing hundreds of Bettye's family photos and select a few that would celebrate her life. The chosen pictures would be copied electronically and displayed at the chapel before her memorial service.

I went into the small office and library in my home and began this task, heavy with emotion because I loved Bettye dearly. It was difficult to sort through all of the images that reflected the events of her life and her beautiful, positive spirit. After many hours of effort, which extended late into that Saturday night, I made the final selections. There were thirty photos, which I then arranged in proper order. I placed them in a small flat box which I laid at the foot of my office recliner. I got out of that recliner, closed the door as I left the room and went directly to bed. Everyone else in the house was already asleep.

Bettye passed away early the next morning. Anyone who has been through it knows the stressful mixture of feelings, confusion and activities that attend these occasions. So many emotional moments, telephone calls, arrangements and details to resolve, all happening at once. So, temporarily, the photos were forgotten.

Early that afternoon, I remembered that I had yet to take the photos to the chapel. I went to my office to get them. I opened the office door, but the small flat box containing the pictures was not there. Everything else was just as I had left it the night before, except the box and its contents had simply vanished.

I searched the room from top to bottom several times--the bookshelves, the cabinets, the box containing the rejects. I searched the rest of the house, even the trash. All to no avail. Was my mind playing tricks on me? In the stress of the moment, had I put them somewhere else and then completely forgotten? I knew I had not, but I had no explanation.

As the day wore on, during free moments, I searched again, every inch of the house. Still nothing. So late that evening, I sat in my office again with the box of rejected pictures, settled again into the same recliner chair, and started the process again. In a couple of hours, I found maybe six potential replacements, one stunning snapshot that was previously overlooked, but that was all. The rest were simply not suitable. I placed those few on my desk, and gave up for the night. I decided I would go through my own accumulated photos the next morning. It had been a long Sunday but time was running out.

When Monday morning came, I was greeted with another list of errands that the circumstances required. Just before noon, with those accomplished, I returned to my office to dig into my storage cabinets in search of more replacements. But when I walked into the room, there, on the floor at the foot of my recliner, was the flat box that had been missing. The box was in precisely the same place I had put it on Saturday night. I wasted no time retrieving it. It contained all the photos that had been missing and they were in same order. I remembered the additional stunning picture of Bettye I had found on Sunday night and added it to others in the small box and hurried off to deliver them to the chapel.

I delivered the eulogy at Bettye's memorial service the next day and I told this story to those assembled. The chapel director said she had never heard anything so unexplainable in her long career.

I struggle often with the mysteries of why we are here, our place in this universe, and the uncertainties of whether we have a spiritual existence that survives our physical presence on this planet. Bettye did not know that struggle. She was not overtly religious, and never confronted others on matters of faith. But she told me once that she trusted that the God who gave her life would be good to her if she was good to Him. For her, it was that simple. There was, for her, no mystery, no struggle.

I don't know exactly where those pictures were while they were missing, but I believe Bettye took them for two purposes: First, because her meticulous spirit wanted to review and approve them; and more importantly, because she wanted to send back a message. She wanted to tell those who loved her that somewhere, perhaps very near to where we are, there is a spiritual reality that follows life as we know it. She wanted to tell us that there is no need to fret about religion and spiritual matters. She wanted to tell each of us to just live and be a good person; and if we do that, we don't have to worry about what comes next.

Mortality

COMING TO GRIPS with one's own mortality is a very personal matter. For me, a natural part of that process is to wonder what the answers are to questions that can only be answered after death claims me.

Usually, it is on a quiet evening, when my mind is otherwise at rest, that I have conversations with myself about these questions - not conversations that other people can hear – but thoughts and counter-thoughts that leave me both intrigued and dismayed. What follows is an example of one of those conversations.

I read somewhere that scientists have concluded that the earliest known humans came into existence about 200,000 years ago. Get your head around that – Two Hundred Thousand years. That conclusion is based upon the testing of skeletal remains containing carbon and genetic data which reveal how long ago the creatures that used those bones died.

It isn't really important whether those bones are the absolute oldest human bones or not. What is important is that our species has been living and dying on this planet for something in the neighborhood of Two Hundred Thousand years, which, in my opinion, is a very long time to be dead. But dead those early humans are, and dead they will remain. Unless...unless...unless there is another life that awaits all human creatures following the occurrence of physical death.

So that brings us right to some critical questions, doesn't it? Questions such as this: What are the chances that we humans are destined to experience a continued non-physical (call it spiritual if you prefer) existence after our lives on this earth end? What could ever justify such a belief in the first place? And if there is such a life after death awaiting humans, what other creatures are included? What about our favorite pets? What about other animals? And bugs, what about bugs?

Then, if there is life for humans after death, where does that take place? Do we get to choose where our heaven is going to be and who we will see there? I, for one, have some very specific people in mind with whom I do not care to spend one more minute. And, of course, there are also some people who are very dear to me, some still alive and some not. I want to be sure I wind up in the same heavenly neighborhood as they do. How does all that work?

What if a person who dies has been a most generous, responsible and kind person with an A+ in all behavior categories during life here on earth, but didn't attend a church or pray because he or she just didn't believe in God? What happens to that person? If that kind of person doesn't receive the same heavenly reward as another person with an A+ who did believe in God, I'm not sure I want to be a part of that kind of system. But I don't want to be left out either. What are my options? Surely, if you've been a good person, there are options.

And what if, like most of us, you've been a pretty good person most of the time, but not perfect – like, for example, what if you have been about a B- person? And what if one of those people you really loved during life on earth was an A+ and you were just a B- or maybe even only a D+? Then what?

See. I have those kinds of conversations with myself all the time. They aren't always the same but they end up with the same result. I give up trying to figure these things out, because no matter what the answers are, I can't do anything about any of it anyway. Then I go to bed.

Jack

OUR DOG, Jack, died last night. He truly was one of a kind – a mixture of breeds unknown. He looked like a golden and brown wolf, but with a more rounded, softer snout.

We knew the end was near, especially during the last 24 hours. He had stopped eating and drinking and didn't move all day from his bed. So when Jack breathed his last, he was not alone. Our son, Layne, was with him, petting and stroking his long soft coat. Then with tears in his eyes, Layne woke me with the news.

Jack was 14 years old last December, the best we can figure. He came to us at a Humane Society in Arizona in October of 99. They said he was 10 months old then. So, if you believe dogs age seven times faster than humans, that means Jack was the equivalent of 106 years old. And guess what – the night before he died, he wanted to go for a walk. So we did – Jack and me – together – just like old times. Not very far. Not very fast. But up and down the street we went, and back up our steep driveway. And Jack was happy.

Jack could talk. He didn't speak English, but he could talk. When he was hungry he uttered a particular "jackspeak" groan that sounded like it should be spelled: "ruoower." When he wanted to investigate the possibility of a walk through the neighborhood, he would tell me "ryerowerow." Most all of his words started with "r." When he would greet me in the garage as I came home from work, I would hear Jack's version of the day's events: "rowerowourowrow" was a common report. It meant everything was cool and he was through managing the family's affairs until tomorrow.

Jack loved young children. If you were a kid under ten or eleven, you could get right up in his face, take his food, pull his hair, and even sit on him, and he would not snap or growl or bark or flinch. But Jack did not like plumbers, electricians or yard workers. Consequently, for the past 14 years, we have had some difficulty convincing those nice people to provide their services at our house. But we worked through it – Jack just spent a little time in "time out" when those folks came around.

Jack was the best watchdog ever.

Jack didn't like rain storms – the kind with thunder and lightning.

Jack loved the coldest days of the year and snow and ice.

Jack did not like electric fences which were intended to keep him in his yard.

Jack most certainly did not like to be bathed or groomed by strangers, and he didn't tolerate anybody – not nobody no how – who proposed to brush his hair while he was conscious.

When Jack died, his spirit went directly to the beautiful person who rescued him and brought him into our family – Ashley Jane Miller.

Lonesome Pop

Evansville Courier & Press
Wednesday, November 17, 1999

RELATIONSHIPS, after all, are what life is all about. Some of us learn that sooner than others. Some learn it too late. Some of us never get it. I don't know when Pop learned it. I know now that he did. But I would never have guessed it in his lifetime.

Pop was my Grandpa. I never heard him speak of love or tenderness. Maybe he thought it unmanly. Maybe it was in those days. Pop had a love story to tell. But he almost never told it. When Pop was 92, he took his love story with him to the grave. And there it remained until my cousin found his letter one recent day.

The Pop I knew was irritable and gruff. He didn't say much to anybody, least of all to squealing grandkids, like me. Maybe it was because he couldn't hear very well anymore. Factory noise had ruined his ears.

When Pop was 11 or 12, he'd had enough of childhood. So he left Posey County to join a traveling circus. He never said much about his life on the road, but after a few years, he came home. A little while later, he met Clara.

Clara's mom didn't like him too much in the beginning. But Clara did, and soon they married. For Clara and the two boys they had together, Pop spent his early adult years in the hot, noisy, grimey factories that eventually stole his hearing. His only respite in those days was a river camp in Union Township where he fished and found some time for Clara.

Then the Depression shut the factories down and the bank took their house, their camp, everything. Pop could only find a job as a janitor. So he took it, and he and Clara struggled on. In those days, she was the one dependable constant in his life. There to take care of him, cook for him and answer to his needs. There for his boys. Always there, working hard and staying the course with him. And together they made it through those lean years to blessed retirement.

Then, suddenly and early in retirement, Clara got sick and soon she was gone. It wasn't supposed to happen that way. But it did. So for twenty years more Pop was left on this earth without her. I don't remember ever seeing him smile after Clara died. Little wonder, now that I've read his letter. He must have been so lonely.

He spent a lot of that time staring out of a window onto Barker Avenue. I would make infrequent visits to see him. When I did, I would wonder what he was thinking about as he looked outside. Now I think I know. Because on one of those countless days he spent alone, Pop found a pen and some paper and summoned every tool that remained from his third grade education. He wanted to write a letter. Maybe the only letter he ever wrote. The envelope said it was to be opened after he died. That's when my cousin found it. Long after he died.

Punctuation and spelling were not Pop's strong suits, but that only made the letter more genuine. He wrote about Clara. It was the love story he'd never told. I think he'd be proud for you to read it, exactly as he wrote it. It says this:

> "if I had My Life to live over again I would search the country until I found the same little girl that I had her name was Clara to me she was the sweetest girl in the world she made me very happy she was a good wife & a good mother for our children she was always ready to do anything to help me all of our many years of married life which was 56 years I loved her with all my heart the only thing I did not show my love as much as I should of done to her we had one last walk together in the Hospital one week before God called her away I will never forget that last walk we had together.
>
> "if I had my life to live over again we would go back to Bradenton Fla and hunt and find Palm village trailer Park where we spent some of our Happiest years of our life together we had so many good friends there I can still see them come in + talk to Clara every day God Bless he sole I know She is in Heaven + I Know it won't be too long before I will meet her again there is not no

woman living that can take Clara's Place with me. Lonesome Pop."

Lonesome Pop. I wish that kind of loneliness and despair didn't have to happen. I wish the rest of us could do something about it. But it is the price a survivor pays for a life of love. I suspect the price is much higher for one who lives a life without such relationships.

I wish Pop would have talked more about his feelings and his pain. But like so many others before and since, he chose not to. I wish Clara could have been there when he wrote his letter. I wish she could have read what he wrote. Then again, maybe she was there; maybe she did read it. Maybe she was in the room at that special moment when he finally let his feelings out and wrote those special words. I hope she was there, looking over his shoulder. Right there – with Lonesome Pop. And maybe he knew it. I hope so.

No. 1. If I had ~~my~~ Life to live over

If I had My Life to live over again I would search the country untill I found the same little girl that I had her name was Clara Sitzman to me she was the sweetest girl in the world she maid very ~~b~~ happy she was a good wife & a good Mother for our children she was always ready to help others to at one time she had her Mother, her Grandfather her Brother & her Neice she had a way of making friends ~~with~~ with her neabors & they all loved her so much she was always ready to do any thing to help me all of our many years of Marred life which was 56 4½ years I loved her with all my heart the only thing I did not show my love as much as I should of done to her we had our last walk togeth in the Hospetle one week before God called her ~~away~~ & will never forget that last walk we had togather

over

Do Not open till
After My Death
Pop

if I had My life to live over

if I had My Life No 2 to live over again we would go back to Bredenton Fla &hunt & find Palm vilage Trailor Park where we spent some of our Happest years of our life togeather we had so many good friends thire & I can still see them come in & talk with Clara every day if My halth as good as it is now as of this note I am writing. I intend to go back thire this fall & thank them in Person for all the nice cards & letters they sent to us she would always smile when I would here is a letter from Palm vilage God Bless her sole & I Know She is in Heaven & I Know it wont be to long before I will meet her again thire is not no woman leaving that can take Claras Place with Me - Lonesum Pop

Marion A. Miller

Beautiful Mother

TONIGHT, when I lay my head down, it will be the first night in my 61 years that my mother is not alive. Not many have their parents for so long. In that, I am fortunate. But tonight, I will struggle with this loss.

It was her time to go, even maybe past her time. I know that. I do not know where she has gone. I am not blessed with her absolute faith in another life. I tell myself that none of us on this side of death can know the answer with certainty. But if there is life after death, my mother lives on in whatever heaven is. And if this life is all there is, then my comfort is in knowing that she lived the life she was given to the full.

I believe that every one of us brings an individual energy into this world. And I believe that we each leave a spiritual presence behind for those who love us when we go. So my mother survives here because her spirit remains, and I will ever feel it.

The winters when I was five and six years old were fierce and brutally cold. My dad traveled often and long in those days. So it was left to my mom and me to go outside into the middle of those nights, and to raise the heavy cellar door that gave access to the furnace room below. We would go down into that cellar, shovel the "klinckers" out from the coal-fired furnace, and shovel in the coal that would keep the house warm overnight. Klinckers were the heavy, craggy, hard residue from the stoker coal that the furnace had burned that day. They would smother the flame if not removed. So we worked together, my mom and I, to get them out and to deliver them into the night. In those days, I was her man when her real man was away.

Then we moved away for a year to a townhouse apartment in Chicago Heights, 30 miles south of the real Chicago. I was in second grade. Dad traveled every week. Until this move, my mother had lived in the same house her entire life, and had always known the fellowship of four close sisters. Now she was alone, pregnant, 33, and without a car, living in a strange place where she knew almost no one except my three year-old sister and me.

It was a tough winter, inside the house and outside. We would walk through the snow to the grocery together, eat together, do everything together. When Dad was gone, mom and I even went to bed together. And on those cold nights, we would sing ourselves to sleep together.

She was a devout Catholic, my mother. So she taught me the hymns of a devout Catholic. Her favorite was "On this day, Oh Beautiful Mother," a hymn to Mary. We sang it every night, and it calmed us, perhaps for different reasons, and brought us rest. Still today, I remember all of the words to that song. But on this day, today, only the title is important.

A few years later, I was a pre-teen with an Evansville Courier paper route. I wanted that paper route. My mom did not. She wanted me home in my bed at the pitch dark hour of 4:30 a.m. and she worried terribly when I left the house to make my rounds. But she never stood in my way.

Then I was a teenager who sometimes required discipline, and soon a college student who only required money. She was there to deliver both. I didn't know then how painful it was for her to watch in silence as her firstborn and then each of my siblings broke away, bit by bit, from her protective cover. But I know now because I have lived that pain myself. Still, she supported me from a distance when I needed her as I made my mistakes and found my place in the world.

Later, there came a time when her religious principles and my own choices brought us to conflict and impasse. The silence between us was short, but agonizing. Her love and trust compelled her to overcome that impasse and accept my decisions. And her horizon grew again in middle age. It was a remarkable and difficult feat for a German Catholic girl born in 1917.

Her health has been failing in recent years. Living 300 miles away made it difficult for me to find the days to visit, and more difficult still to know if a health crisis she perceived as real was, in fact, real. As time passed, she focused more and more on her physical troubles whenever I would call. Some were real, some were not, but all were born of the fear inherent in aging. There were many false alarms.

But her broken hip two years ago was real. A diagnosis of Parkinson's was real. An open-heart by-pass surgery was real. And more recently, there was a real tumor in her stomach. Through all this, she fought to live, because she loved life and people.

On what would be her final weekend, my wife and I drove to Michigan to see her. There was something spiritual about my decision to make that trip. Travel and business commitments had consumed most of my recent months. I had not seen Mom since Thanksgiving. Then, ten days before she died, as I moved about the country, I called on a cell phone to talk with her. I was tired of being on the road and intended to spend the next weekend at home with my wife and kids. But during that phone call, without ever asking me to come, she summoned me. I knew, instinctively, that I had to get there on that next weekend. So I did.

And on that last Saturday night of her life, we celebrated my 61st birthday together. Mom and I sat at the long oval dinner table with my Dad, my sister and brothers and their spouses and children – the same table where for a half-century we shared so many other special meals. Mom smiled at us through desperate eyes that told me this would never happen again. We talked and laughed and sang the birthday song. And I blew out the candles and we ate the cake and ice cream. She had as much fun that night as her frail body would permit, with all the family she so loved. And, always the night owl, she was the last to go to bed.

The next day, before we departed, she lamented that she felt so weak and she wondered aloud, "How did I ever get in this hole?" I hugged her for a long moment and told her I would be back to see her again very soon, but I knew, or thought I knew, that even sooner, she would be gone. She told me how good I looked in my new shirt and sweater and she kissed me on the cheek. And I kissed her. She told me she loved me. She said "Bye, Sweetie." I remember thinking that nobody else could get away with calling me "Sweetie." But she could. Then we left.

Tomorrow, I will go back to her house. This time she won't be there to kiss me. She will be everywhere and nowhere. So on this day, Beautiful Mother, I want you to know this: Whenever a soft breeze brushes my cheek, it will be your spirit reminding me of your gentle touch. And I will greet your spirit silently with that same song in my mind that we sang so many times, so close together, so long ago, when a little boy and his mother needed each other so much. And just as I did then, I will say to you, "I love you, Mom."

(David Miller's mother died in Michigan on March 25, 2004. He wrote this remembrance on the evening of that day.)

Grieving For a Lost Daughter

I CAN ONLY describe it from the perspective of a dad.

I have grieved until I was exhausted and I could grieve no more. Then I grieved again and yet again. I have stared into the evening sky and wondered where she is among the stars. I have cried and ached and lay awake at night. I imagine her final moments alone in that wreckage and each time I feel physically sick and helpless and sad and hopeless. Even though years have passed, that still happens. Over those years, I have put the flame to thousands of candles by the urn that holds her ashes. I have spoken to her spirit more than once every day. And still, she is out there somewhere and I remain here. I long to see her and kiss her cheek, but I cannot.

I have seen her profile in her daughter's sleeping face. I have held that child in my arms and imagined her mother's presence there. I have disciplined that child and I knew in that moment that I was her mother's voice. And still, I feel her spirit out there somewhere in the universe, but I do not know what a spirit is, and I cannot touch her.

I see her in photographs. I see her in my mind and in my dreams. But I cannot see her, really. I sense her presence next to me at times, while walking the dog or when I am alone—like now. My eyes cannot see her, but still, I know she is there, somewhere, and I wonder where "somewhere" is, and I wonder how and when I am going to get there.

I miss her every day. Deep in the marrow of my being, I miss her. The emotional wound is open and permanent. When my mind fixes directly upon the reality that she is not here, in those moments my head shakes an involuntary "no." and I sigh, and that feeling returns to the pit of my stomach – that same feeling that came upon me the day it happened – that empty, sickening feeling of utter despair that comes with the realization that I will not – that I cannot – see her or touch her, ever again. No, it never ends. Nor do I want it ever to end.

Now that I have described my experience as a father, go back and read this one more time. And while you do that, imagine the ten-fold pain of my daughter's best friend – her mother.

Ashley's Graduation

I T IS NOT MY HABIT to plan personal travel very far in advance. But for almost a year, May 9, 2008, had been blocked out for a trip to Arizona to attend my daughter's law school graduation ceremony. As soon as she told me that date, I vowed that nothing would keep me away – nothing.

I was there in the auditorium at the appointed time, just as I had planned. She was there too, but not for others to see, or to congratulate, or to hug. Not in the way anybody had planned. She was there within me and within her brother, Andrew, who was with me. And the strength that her spirit gave us carried us through that day.

From the moment God called her home, I had known it would be a difficult moment when her name was called and I walked in her stead to accept her diploma. But I also knew that somehow, she had to be present for this. She deserved to be present. And the only way that could now happen was for me to carry her spirit there.

I had long ago resolved, in spite of my grief, that this recognition of our precious child, who succeeded both in motherhood and in academia, should be an occasion to celebrate – not to mourn. Nevertheless, I knew that the mixture of pride and sadness that I would feel that day would inevitably bring some tears.

We arrived early and were seated at the very end of the first row of spectators so that, when the time came, I could slip into the line of graduates as they proceeded to the stage. We were handed a program. Merely reading it drew the first tears. It said simply that I would accept the diploma for Ashley, and for her daughter, Layla.

I never will be able fully to describe the emotional roller coaster I rode through that ceremony. I remember wondering where she would have been in the line as the graduates were filing in. I was filled with wistful pride when the Dean and a student speaker both spoke of Ashley in their remarks.

When the speeches were over, the graduates' names were called as each crossed the stage. Several of them spoke to me as they passed. When it was time for me to take her place in the line, I took some deep breaths and mounted the stairs. When her name was called, I walked across the stage and the tears came. Through them I watched the faculty on the stage stand and applaud in her honor. There were sincere hugs from the Dean and from a couple of the others who had so recently led Ashley's final classes. They, too, had tears.

The Dean handed me the diploma and I walked down the stairs. As I crossed back in front of the stage, the entire graduating class stood applauding. I raised Ashley's diploma high in the air and there came the most magnificent roar. Then I hugged my waiting son and sat down.

It was the longest one-minute walk of my life. But it was a precious walk with Ashley. I felt her strength and presence in every step I took, and for those few seconds, she and I were one. It was her graduation, but I received the gift. I will keep the memory of it forever.

If two people love each other, there can be no happy end to it. Ernest Hemingway, Death in the Afternoon *(1932)*

<u>Ashes</u>

I WILL NEVER forget that weekend in May, 2004. My mother had died in March. So in early May I drove back to St. Joseph, Michigan, for a weekend visit with my Dad. He was 87 and, after 60 years of marriage, he was struggling with grief and his newly imposed solitude. He was so glad to have me visit and there was evidence of his effort to be positive and a good host. He had gone to the grocery to get in some snack foods and drinks. Had he not done that, the shelves would have been bare.

As ever before, the old Victorian house creaked and otherwise spoke its age when night fell, as the wind off Lake Michigan, two blocks away, hit the coast line. And during that evening, as ever before, our conversation was light and easy. Nothing memorable. We talked about children, grandchildren and great-grandchildren. We watched the TV news and Letterman and we listened to music. We did not talk about my mother.

The next day, we visited with my sister and brothers, had lunch at a local pub and otherwise wiled away the day. A disinterested outsider would have concluded that nothing important was being accomplished that weekend. But that would be wrong. I thought of it then, and still do today, as precious time spent with a precious man whose life had a new, gaping hole in it that would never be filled. When I left on Sunday to return to my home in Southern Indiana, he thanked me for coming at least 10 times.

I would repeat those weekend visits with my dad at least three or four times each year until 2010 when he passed away, apparently in his sleep, at age 93. And every one of those weekends was filled with the same easy love and laidback companionship. We just "hung out" together, that's all.

During that first visit, after dinner on Saturday evening, dad asked me if I would go with him the next morning to visit mom's mausoleum. Of course I said I would. The next morning, Dad was extremely quiet during the drive to the cemetery. And for the first ten or so minutes, while we stood beneath the crypt bearing her name, nothing was said – not one word by from either of us. He seemed to be traveling mentally in another world.

Then, with his head bowed and his eyes closed, my dad reached up and pressed his hand against her nameplate which was about a foot above his head. He was literally leaning on the stone covering of her resting place. He was positioned as though he was waiting for a bus. After a few more minutes passed, I said to him: "She's not in there, Dad. She's in heaven." And without hesitation, head still bowed, he responded: "Something is in there." And then he walked to the car.

I never mentioned that event to my dad again, but I never forgot it either. And for a few years, the helplessness and grief embedded in his simple response haunted me from time to time. Then, one horrible day in 2007, I came to know exactly what he meant – the emotion he was feeling – and why he said what he said.

The ashes of my daughter, Ashley, who died in an automobile accident in 2007, now reside in an urn in my home office. The urn is sterling silver and is enshrined among candles and memories and photos I have placed there. Every day, when I first arise – yes, every day – I go to that place in my home and I stand there in silence, sometimes for several minutes, in exactly the same emotional state of contemplation as my dad experienced on that Sunday morning when I drove him to the mausoleum. Then I light those candles, and I place my hands around that urn, and I speak silently to Ashley's spirit. And I try in vain to fill that gaping hole in my heart that will never ever heal. I know that Ashley is not in that urn. But I also know that my Dad was right on that Sunday morning in May.

"Something" – something forever sacred – "is in there."

If I Could

GEORGE CARLIN was among the most creative comedians of the late 20th century. One example of his genius was his creation and delivery of how great it would be if we could live our lives backwards. George reasoned that if we did live life backwards, we could get death out of the way first. Then we would experience improving health and strength during the elderly period and have the most adult fun early in life when we would have maximum size and energy. Then, eventually, we would be completely cared for as an infant and finish up life as an orgasm. What a way to go!

George didn't learn how to create and deliver that quality of humor in school or by reading a book. He was born with "talent" that, at some point in his life, refused suppression.

In interviews, George reported that his talent came out of him almost without any effort – sometimes spontaneously. Often, the idea was just "there in his head" for him to seize and preserve.

The same kind of experience was described more than once by singer-songwriter, John Denver, who conceived and created one of his greatest hits, "Annie's Song," during a ten minute ride on a ski lift.

Artists are gifted with meaningful visions and brains specially equipped to create sources of sensory enjoyment. Topping my list of favorites are visual artists who create objects pleasing to the eye and provocative to the brain, those who compose well-written musical pieces embedded with insightful messages and performing artists, such as Carlin, who can make us think and laugh at the same time. I would love to do that . . . if I could.

There is, however, the small matter of the required creative talent. That is to say, I have none. I cannot draw; I cannot paint a picture with a brush. I have never been able to compose music or play a musical instrument. And I would be "hooked" off the stage if I attempted stand-up comedy.

True works of art and artistic performances, however, often do more than grab and hold our attention because of their sensual magnetism. They speak to us. They are vehicles of truth, of caution or challenge or love that stay with us long after the moments when we encounter them.

Artists frequently are influential catalysts of enormous social, cultural or governmental change. One familiar and undeniable example of this phenomenon is the Edna Ferber novel, "Showboat," which in 1927 became a Broadway musical composed by Jerome Kern and Oscar Hammerstein II. This work of literature, musical stage and later, in 1951, an award-winning motion picture, was instrumental in giving birth to the civil rights movement of the 1950's and 1960's. By its spoken lines, its lyrics and story, "Showboat" challenged the racial inequalities and prejudice that permeated America during the first half of the 20th century. It is fair to wonder how much longer that movement would have been delayed without the overtones and the not-so-subtle admonitions of "Showboat."

If there is a lesson to take from the modest level of appreciation Americans have for the power of art to reshape our nation and our world, it is this: Artists are a different breed. They feel, they smell, they taste and they see the same world as the rest of us, but they experience that world in an intensely different way. They might as well be on a different planet. That is why they can speak to the rest of us about re-examining our priorities, about what is on the horizon and what is really happening to us and around us.

"Artistic talent" comes in two basic varieties: Creative talent and performing talent. Both involve an uncanny combination of abilities to sense and understand the significance of some condition or event when the rest of us cannot, and then bring something into existence that communicates to us the beauty, danger, wisdom, injustice or tragedy of that condition or event.

That combination of a unique sensitivity to recognize otherwise unseen dimensions, along with the ability to communicate and describe those dimensions in music or speech or in images painted or drawn, is part of the DNA of every true artist. It cannot be taught and it cannot be eliminated from the artist's being.

Do such people sometimes behave in bizarre ways? Yes. Do they sometimes annoy the majority? Yes. Are many of them prophets who are the harbingers of things to come? Yes. Is that a good and sufficient reason for us to listen carefully for their messages? Yes. Yes. A thousand times – Yes.

And would I pay a king's ransom to be one of them? Yes. If I could.

Want a Job?

"**HELP WANTED** - Only the most honorable and selfless, unmarried, never-divorced men need apply. Women are not eligible. Nine full years of unpaid training required before first assignment. Training will occur at a controlled in-residence scholastic institution requiring a rigorous study schedule and limited social contacts. No dating during nine year training period or thereafter.

"After graduation, working hours will vary. Employee should expect to work at least 60 hours every week. Employee will be subject to emergency call at all times. All Sundays and every Christmas Eve, Christmas Day and New Year's Day will be workdays.

"Job responsibilities will include complete business management and direction of large, multi-purpose branch locations. Each branch location has hundreds of members expecting personal attention from the employee on unpredictable, as-needed basis. Employee's duties will also include school administration, social services to poor families, frequent performance of rituals, teaching, individual counseling, family counseling, marriage counseling, crisis management, fund raising, frequent public speaking, providing comfort to the sick and dying and to the families of the sick and dying, conflict resolution, social services director, youth activities coordinator, confessor and youth sports organizer and coach.

"Salary less than minimum wage and below the government-defined poverty level. No overtime pay no matter what. Advancement possible, but without salary increase. Applicant will be expected to participate in various civic organizations and to perform various additional services in the community for free and without expectation of compensation. Retirement benefits negligible. Reward, if any, only comes in heaven, if any.

"Absolute and unquestioning compliance with employer's policies and directives required at all times. Failure to meet this standard may result in unpleasant and/or solitary work assignments.

"Employee will normally be required to live alone in quarters selected and owned by employer, and to move from one community to another at direction of employer every few years. Saintly standard of daily behavior will be expected of employee by entire community. If employee commits even a minor infraction of civil law, public embarrassment out of all proportion to the violation is assured.

"Job also requires ironclad agreements by employee to remain unmarried for entire life, and never to have any sexual relationship whatsoever at any time. No exceptions. Recent developments require that employee must NEVER give anyone a hug or otherwise touch another person, lest employee be accused of sexual misconduct. Loneliness and isolation are guaranteed.

"Any man interested in making an application should first undergo extensive psychiatric analysis. If still interested after that, contact the Catholic Bishop in your diocese or dial 1-888-IAM-NUTS."

Is there anybody out there who wants to be a Catholic priest?

The most beautiful and deepest experience a [person] can have is a sense of the mysterious. [One] who never had this experience seems to me, if not dead, then at least blind. To sense that behind anything that can be experienced there is a something that our mind cannot grasp and whose beauty and sublimity reaches us only indirectly and as a feeble reflection, this is religiousness. In this sense I am religious. To me it suffices to wonder at these secrets and to attempt humbly to grasp with my mind a mere image of the lofty structure of all that there is.

– Albert Einstein, *"The World As I See It" (1949)*

Human Connection (Einstein)

LATE IN HIS LIFE, Albert Einstein wrote: "What an extraordinary situation is that of us mortals! Each of us is here for a brief sojourn; for what purpose we know not, though sometimes we think we feel it. From the point of view of daily life, we exist for our fellow-men – in the first place for those upon whose smiles and welfare all our happiness depends, and next for all those unknown to us personally with whose destinies we are bound up."

Thus did this genius acknowledge that our lives cannot be solitary, nor can our daily decisions be based exclusively on our own selfish interests. We are defined as individuals by our relationships with those who love us. We are defined as a people by our relationships with other nations.

Einstein believed in a God whose existence is defined by the orderliness of the universe and its physical laws – a God who does not intervene in the daily affairs of human life. If he was right, and I believe he was, that leaves us on our own to bear the responsibility for, and the consequences of, our own individual and collective conduct.

Even if Einstein's view of the absence of daily divine intervention is wrong, it is undeniable that we are vested with broad discretion over our own behavior, both personal and collective. We exercise that discretion every day in the conduct of our personal relationships, and we thereby cause either good or ill in our own lives and the lives of others.

That was Einstein's point. Our personal relationships with those with whom we live and communicate everyday are at the center of our being. We cannot completely avoid those relationships, even if we try. Nor can we escape the consequences embedded within them.

Ernest Hemingway wisely observed: "If two people love each other, there can be no happy end to it." And he was right. Consequently, some among us fear the bonds, the responsibilities and the risks that are inherent in close, loving relationships. Indeed, those bonds, responsibilities and risks are the costs of loving. Nevertheless, the internal reward that comes from knowing the love of a friend, a child or a spouse cannot be denied. It is a pleasure without which living is only existing.

Likewise, there are people who refuse to acknowledge the basic human need for casual social interaction. Unlike commitments involving love, social relationships carry with them few responsibilities and minimal risk of emotional pain. Nevertheless, for reasons known only to themselves, many people resist mixing with strangers or inviting new friendships. In doing so, they deprive themselves of opportunities to experience the kindnesses, the support, the networking and the genuine caring that new social relationships can offer.

My messages to you are these: Close relationships are treasures that will provide comfort in the worst of times. Do not be afraid to love no matter your age or circumstance. Do not be afraid to intertwine your life and your future with those who genuinely love you. And mix with people. You may rediscover yourself in the process. Mutual dependence for some part of life's happiness is not a commitment to be feared. Rather, it is a recognition that our welfare depends upon our willingness to live and to love together.

Sermons

SOME PEOPLE can inspire and move an audience with their speeches and sermons. Most cannot. Many of those who cannot, however, refuse to admit that they cannot and continue to victimize the rest of us whenever and wherever they can. One of my most earnest wishes is that those who cannot do it well would all be required to leave the speeches and sermons to those who can upon pain of contracting permanent, incurable laryngitis.

At this church I attend on some Sundays, there is this one very nice cleric who simply cannot give a worthwhile sermon. There is another there who can and frequently does. It is like playing a modified form of Russian Roulette when I decide to attend there. Because if one picks the wrong Sundays, you can listen to the worst sermons the Supreme Being could possibly tolerate.

You can if you want to. I don't want to. I've tried; I really have. My mother taught me when I was very small to respect without question those commissioned to sermonize. I just didn't get the "without question" part. I'll probably go to hell. But hell can't be any worse than some of those sermons. Oh well. I'll take my chances.

So anyway, one recent Sunday, there he was. Sermonizing in the worst way, as only he can. I was buried in the middle of a pew full of ladies who seemed hypnotized. They were like my mother. Unquestioning. I speculated to myself that if this audience were not semi-captive and extremely polite, there would probably be no audience at all. And I remembered that this guy has the two worst attributes of all bad speakers – he thinks he's really good and he thinks what he is saying is really important. As a result, he goes on and on and on, the more to thrill and delight his fans. I was not in the mood to endure this, not this day.

Sermons should be short and pithy and to the point. They should be about life and how it relates to the lessons in the holy books. They should be about harmony with our world or harmony in our world. They should be about how to commune with our private God. They don't have to be pleasant but they ought to be relevant. At least relevant. And short – always short. This unfortunate cleric's sermons, however, are none of that. They are, instead, long and labored and repetitious and about nothing that matters. They chase people away from spirituality because if his words are what faith and spirituality are all about, not very many people of the 90s will want a ticket. As the world we live in and its social norms change, the approach to religious discussion must change. Otherwise, religion, for a whole lot of people, becomes irrelevant, boring nothingspeak. And the sad part is that's what most people who seek religious guidance get all dressed up on Sunday to go listen to.

There's a woods near this church. About three minutes into this sermon-without-meaning -or-end on this particular Sunday, the woods called me. No one else could hear it, but the woods called nonetheless. I got up, stumbled across the hypnotized ladies, and walked out into the fresh air, God's air. It was a nice day outside the church, and it was so . . . so spiritual. Something I couldn't see took me behind the church and into the woods, to a long-dead tree trunk laying on its side maybe fifty yards deep into the brush. I sat down there. For thirty minutes or so, I sat and breathed God's air and looked around and enjoyed the quiet that nature offers. Part of the time, I watched a small spider on a leaf near my feet. Part of the time, I watched a squirrel, and part of the time I studied a little twig that I found on the ground. It was the best thirty minutes I've spent with God in a long, long time.

All the sounds there were gentle. They were God's sounds. Birds and the breeze and the rustle of leaves – those kinds of sounds. I didn't need bread and wine there to commune with God. I was as close to Him as I could get. It might have been as close to him as I'll ever get. And I didn't have to listen to that stupid sermon to get that close. It was all accidental. If I would ever consciously try to recreate those minutes, it wouldn't work. But someday, when the sermon stinks again, as it most surely will, and when the birds are at play and the breeze is just right and the squirrels are at work, I'll go back there and sit down in the quiet on that tree trunk and just see what happens.

Maybe I'll get close to Him again. One thing is for sure. I can't do it in a church when nothingspeak prevails.

I Will Probably Go to Hell for Saying this, but...

WHEN I WAS A KID, I knew what we were having for dinner by the days of the week. We had a weekly menu at my house. It almost never changed. Sunday was fried chicken. Monday was pork roast. Tuesday was meat loaf, and so on through the week. Friday was fish.

We were Catholic. My parents said so. They said I would go straight to hell for sure, no questions asked, if I ate meat on a Friday. Even by mistake. Zero tolerance. Then God eliminated that rule in about 1962. The pope told us.

When I heard this news, I was happy for sure. But I couldn't help wondering about all those people who had been otherwise pretty good but got sent to hell because they ate meat on a Friday before 1962. I mean, man, think about it. How do you think all those condemned people felt? The pope picks 1962 to announce that God doesn't care about that meatless Fridays rule anymore. Why not 1942? Or 1742? Or why not just say it was all a big mistake and that any Catholic who ever went to hell because of that rule would have his case reviewed? But no. That was not how it came down. The announcement simply was that the old rule was abolished and that any catholic person who hadn't died yet could eat meat on Friday. I couldn't help thinking that something was not right about this whole thing.

The meatless Friday rule never made any sense anyway, except maybe to commercial fishermen. But my mother said rules for Catholics didn't have to make sense. Like celibacy for priests doesn't make sense. She said if the pope said it was a rule that was the end of the matter.

So, if you were Catholic and you ate a hot dog on a Friday in, say, 1939, and you walked away from the hot dog stand and forgot to look both ways and got run over by a truck before you could go to confession and be forgiven, too bad Jack – eternal damnation, even if you were a very good person, and even if your name was Mother Theresa. No appeals. On the other hand, if you weren't Catholic in 1939, but you were otherwise a good person, and if you ate a hot dog on the same day and then you got hit by the same truck, you got to go straight to heaven. Do not pass "Go," do not collect $200. Straight to heaven. Because, they said, people who weren't Catholic just didn't know "any better." Any better than what? So it didn't seem right, even before the rule was changed.

For example, what about my Grandpa Greif? He died in 1945. I didn't know him very well because I was only two when his number was up. But I have it on good authority that he was a pretty good guy, even though he had more than a few beers during his life. He had nine kids for heaven's sake. Nine. And he was German to the core. Give him a break. At least he didn't go back to Germany. If you had to choose between going home to nine kids and their mother or going home to the Nazis, who would you pick?

In those days, when a hard-working German gentleman had a few beers, it was often Friday. And all of his Lutheran friends could have a fresh hot wienerschnitzel to wash their beers down. I am told that Grandpa Grief did too. Surely that's not grounds for hell without parole. But that was the rule.

I have tried to imagine the conversation that transpired between my Grandpa Greif and St. Peter at the Pearly Gates regarding this subject:

Peter: Hello George.
George: Hello Peter, good to see you.
Peter: Well, yes George, it's nice to see you too; but why are you here?
George: I'm here because I'm dead, Peter. So let me in. My wife is in there.
Peter: Oh, I'm sorry, George, but you can't come in because you ate wienerscnitzel on Fridays with your Lutheran buddies.
George: Say What? But my Lutheran buddies are all in there too. Why would you keep me out?
Peter: You ate wienerschnitzel on a Friday while you were alive, George. You

	were Catholic, but your friends were not. So that was a mortal sin for you, but not for them. You can't come in.
George:	I'll whip your ass; what do you mean I can't come in? I raised nine kids; I went to mass every week and sometimes more; I never cheated on my wife, I supported my parish and gave alms to the poor. I'm a better guy than any of those Lutherans. Get outta my way, Peter.
Peter:	George, make it easy on yourself. I have the power to smite you. That would be unnecessarily painful. You ate meat on a Friday. You knew how evil that was. There are no excuses. You must go now to spend eternity in hell because that's the rule.
George:	Peter, wait. There's a rumor down on earth that God is gonna change that rule. Could you check that out before I leave, please?
Peter:	Ha! Nice try, George. God never makes a mistake, so He never changes his mind. A rule is a rule. Go away and stay away.

Now that would have been in 1945, when my Grandpa died. Here, I guess, is the conversation between George and Peter in late 1962, when the rule changed:

George: Hey, Peter. Do you have a minute? What am I saying? You have an eternity.

Peter: What is it George? It is highly irregular for me to have any contact with people already in hell.

George: Well, yeah, that's what I wanted to talk to you about, Peter. Do you remember why you made me go to hell?

Peter: Of course I do. It was because you ate meat on Friday.

George: That's right, Peter. But look down there on earth now, all the Catholics are allowed to eat meat on Fridays. God changed the rule. If it's okay for Catholics to do that now, why was it wrong when I was alive, Peter? I think you should reconsider and let me into heaven now.

Peter: Don't be silly, George. I can't do that. When you ate meat on Friday, it was a mortal sin. Just because it isn't a mortal sin anymore doesn't mean that somebody who committed a mortal sin in 1939 gets it erased. The rule is that if a person commits a mortal sin while alive, and if that mortal sin is not properly forgiven, that person goes to hell. You know

	that rule, George. God never changes His mind.
George:	But Peter, don't you see the problem with that logic?
Peter:	George, you're a Catholic. What's logic got to do with it?

The Real Story of Adam and Eve

MANY PEOPLE around the world have believed for centuries, and some still believe, that it all began about 5,000 years ago. According to one rather famous Book, that was when a man named "Adam" let his new live-in companion, whose name was "Eve," talk him into doing something really stupid.

The Book says that Adam was new to the area, which was called the "Garden of Eden." In fact, the Book says that Adam had recently been made – yes, I said "made" – by a Mysterious Invisible Spirit who talked with Adam from time to time. So Adam was fairly young. He had no experience in dealing with women because the Book makes it clear there were no women until Eve. And Adam had no formal education, because he had never attended school. At that time, according to the Book, there were no schools at all.

What we know about Eve is that she was a little bit younger than Adam and she was made by the same Mysterious Invisible Spirit out of spare parts taken back from Adam without Adam's permission while Adam was asleep.

Nobody knows for sure exactly what the stupid thing was that Adam and Eve did. But we all have our personal suspicions. And the reasons for those suspicions are many. The Book describes this "something stupid" event as involving an irresistible desire felt by both Adam and Eve, but Eve's persuasion convinced Adam to do it with her. The Book also says this event took place when Adam and Eve didn't have any clothes on. They were both completely naked the entire time.

Now, when a boy and a girl are naked together for a sustained period of time, they are most usually "up to something." Everybody knows that. And the Book says that when the Mysterious Invisible Spirit caught up with Adam and Eve and asked them about the stupid thing they did in the Garden of Eden, they admitted doing it together, and both Adam and Eve were very embarrassed and they "covered themselves." And then the Mysterious Invisible Spirit was pretty upset and he threw them out of the Garden. You don't get embarrassed and put clothes on for the very first time ever and get thrown out of your home if you are only caught eating an apple.

Perhaps we should analyze this situation in a little more detail. All of the events described in the Book that took place before Adam and Eve did whatever "stupid thing" they did was the handiwork of the Mysterious Invisible Spirit. First, the Book says, he made the heavens and the earth. Then he said, "Let there be light," and there was light. Just so you understand that, it says right there in the Book that he made the heavens and the earth in the dark, which immediately raises some questions about the organizational skills of the Mysterious Invisible Spirit.

So then the same Spirit made a new rule. However, he didn't have any people who had to follow his new rule. So then he made Adam, who had no input into the rule and no training about how to follow the rule but apparently, Adam couldn't break the rule all by himself. Then, as a matter of pure coincidence, a short time later, Adam complained that he was lonely and he needed a companion. Adam probably had in mind finding a buddy with whom he could hunt and gather.

And that is when the Mysterious Invisible Spirit decided to make Eve. But he didn't bother to discuss the matter with Adam in advance. He just put Adam to sleep and went to work. When he finished making Eve, he left her sleeping right there next to Adam for a while. Then he woke them up and, at that moment, the first man and the first woman saw one another for the first time, and they were both naked. It seems to have been kind of like the ultimate blind date.

According to the Book, it was under those exact circumstances that the Mysterious Invisible Spirit first told Adam and Eve about his new rule. The Book says the rule involved not eating the fruit from a certain tree. Nobody believes that. However, it is clear that Adam and Eve were forbidden to do something that the Mysterious Invisible Spirit knew Adam and Eve would want very badly to do.

At that point, according to the Book, the Mysterious Invisible Spirit went away, leaving Adam and Eve alone to frolic in the Garden together. This was obviously a pretty irresponsible thing for a parent or guardian to do – allowing a couple of immature young adults to run the neighborhood unsupervised with no clothes on. But that's what the Book says happened. They didn't even know the name or address of the Mysterious Invisible Spirit, or where he hung out, or how to get in touch with him if they needed help or had an important question. He would just show up – well, not really "show up," because he was invisible – at random times to check on Adam and Eve, which also seems a little creepy when you think about it.

The Book doesn't say where the making of Adam took place, nor the exact location of the Garden of Eden. However, the Book does report that the Mysterious Invisible Spirit made Adam first, and that Adam was made exactly "in his own image." It seems fair to ask how that works, because the last time I checked, nobody can see an invisible presence. So, since the Mysterious Invisible Spirit was not visible, he wouldn't have had an image to copy.

In any event, when the Mysterious Invisible Spirit was finished making Adam, he placed Adam on this planet – the Earth. Now try to understand this. There are more than one hundred billion galaxies in the universe, each consisting of billions and billions of related stars, and planets. Yet he plopped Adam down on this relatively tiny planet we call "Earth" – a speck of place in space where the Mysterious Invisible Spirit knew trouble and diseases and wars would afflict the population with regularity for centuries. So why on earth would he pick Earth? But that's what the Book says.

So when Adam woke up after the Mysterious Invisible Spirit swiped his rib to make Adam's newly designated significant other, Eve, there she was, laying right next to him. Adam was undoubtedly very surprised by this development. Eve was already made, and she was Adam's responsibility. Moreover, she was not the hunting and gathering guy that Adam had in mind. She was not a guy at all. Without any prior notice to Adam, there she was, small and soft and needing Adam's support and protection. Worst of all, she could already talk and she immediately wanted Adam's constant attention.

Adam's first instinct when he took in all the detail was very likely something like: "Run Adam, Run!!" But, of course, he was a new arrival himself and didn't know his way around. So he couldn't run away. Besides that, he couldn't sit down and think through his options because Eve wouldn't leave him alone.

Of course, Eve, too, was probably pretty shocked and upset at how things were unfolding. Here she was, meeting her life mate for the first time – it was sort of her wedding day – and she did not have a thing to wear . . . literally. So she complained immediately to (who else?) helpless Adam, as only a woman can.

Adam, in addition to being sorely disappointed that he still didn't have a hunting and gathering buddy, which continued to be his principal concern, now had a hysterical woman in his face demanding that he "Do Something!!!" Adam had no experience to draw upon and no mentor to advise him how to handle this woman. So when Adam couldn't take it anymore, he did something, or they did something which apparently violated the Mysterious Invisible Spirit's rule – which rule both Adam and Eve had forgotten about anyway sometime during their violation of the rule. The Book doesn't say this, but Adam and Eve lived happily ever after. And the rest is history.

And where was the Mysterious Invisible Spirit while all this was happening? The Spirit who had set all this up? Nobody knows and the Book doesn't say. He was just gone. He returned long enough to run Adam and Eve off from his Garden of Eden and to punish a talking snake, but since then he has left the planet and us, its inhabitants, to fend for ourselves. And there has been from that day forward an ongoing disagreement among us about what is in the rule book.

Two Views of the Universe

Evansville Courier & Press
Friday, April 16, 1999

SOMETIMES, in quiet moments, the insignificance of a human being measured against the enormity of this universe is bothersome to me. At the same time, I know there is great potential in each of us. It's a paradox and a source of continuing wonder.

From one perspective, we are specs in space and time. Billions like us have come and gone, and so it will be after us, probably for tens of thousands of years. In that sense, the human race is a very small factor in an incomprehensibly large and enduring place.

Yet, from the other perspective, here we are, at the top of the food and brain chain on this planet at this moment. And we have all been given a gift. We each get only one--but we do get one--a single, finite, precious life to live. And within it there is the vast potential, while we're here, to think, to experience, to smile, to love, to touch, to feel, to understand and, yes, to wonder.

Once I heard a man in his seventies explain his decision to go snow skiing for the first time. "We're here so short and we're gone so long," he said. And so we are.

Only a fool doesn't embrace and fill up every day he's given.

From a theological perspective, if there is a God, and I believe there is, then the greatest sin in His eyes must be wasting the time that He gives us here. And if there is not a god; if the theologians have it all wrong; it's still only makes sense to seize every opportunity for the experiences and relationships life offers, just like the old skier. Because, if there's no god, this life is all there is. There is nothing else.

So, in the end, our awesome insignificance in the larger universe makes no difference. It is just something that is so. What is important is how we each use the smaller universe of life. Unless we are determined to be fools, we have no choice in the matter. Our mission should be to do whatever we can within the bounds of kindness and civility, with and for whomever we can, including ourselves, and to fill up our lives with experiences and relationships.

The key and the limitation is all in that one phrase: "Whatever we can." There are only so many people whose lives we can touch in the time we're given. There are only so many experiences that we can have. There are only so many ideas that we can understand or influence and a limited number of things we can do or achieve. But there are exactly that many of each. So we should expect at least that much of ourselves, and nothing less. If we take that approach, our significance in the universe is huge, because we are each our own universe.

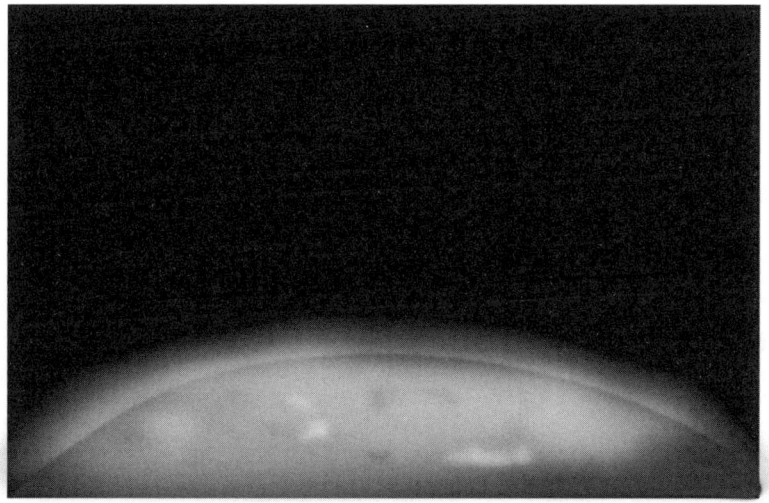

Galaxies

I. Questions

ONE WAY to appreciate the significant limits of our current knowledge and, at the same time, grow ideas and thought processes that are otherwise mere seeds in our brains is to ask ourselves a stream of questions for which we presently have no answers. Consider, for example, the wonders and mysteries of the universe, the spiritual unknowns of its origin. It is where this discussion will begin. Where it will take us is anybody's guess.

What is known by scientists with reasonable certainty about the universe can fairly be compared to a single grain of sand on an endless beach. So we begin with that. Astronomers now estimate that there are at least 100 billion galaxies in our universe. Astronomers say they managed, with the help of the Hubbell telescope, to determine the approximate number of galaxies that occupy the universe and that number is at least 100 billion.

At some point, we have to trust somebody, right? So for purposes of this discussion, we will trust the astronomers. 100 billion galaxies it is. Now, just try to get your brain around that one premise. Not 100 billion planets. Not 100 billion stars. But 100 billion galaxies. And that number is considered to be very conservative.

A galaxy is enormous. Each galaxy consists of millions of stars. Maybe even billions. The late Carl Sagan, who knew more about the universe than the rest of us combined, once said there are more stars in the universe than the number of grains of sand on the earth. That is a lot, even if Sagan missed it by half. So, if there are millions, maybe billions, of stars in each galaxy, there certainly are many billions, and perhaps maybe even trillions, of stars in the entire universe.

At this early stage, we have only mentioned that there are spiritual issues to consider, but it is legitimate to wonder where the hell (no pun intended) all the gases and other materials required to make all those stars and the planets that orbit them came from. We can also ask how the stars ended up where they are. We might even wonder if there is a "where" in the universe. Everywhere may be "nowhere" except by reference to another heavenly body that is also "nowhere." I wonder. But assuming that "where" is a legitimate concept in the context of the universe, there must be a way to calculate the mathematical coordinates of every star and planet relative to…say…our sun. And then we would have to ask how all those stars ended up where they are. And, of course, since "where they are" is constantly and forever changing, you might want to wonder, simultaneously, where the stars started from, where they have been and where they are going.

Returning to something closer to home, this is a good place to acknowledge the relative insignificance of our own size and the size of our own planet. Compared to other stars, our sun, which is itself a star, is small to medium in size. And revolving around our sun in various orbits are at least eight planets, including the one we live on and call "Earth." Our sun and our Earth are very small pieces of the galaxy they occupy, which we call the "Milky Way." And we, the humans who inhabit this planet Earth (each for a very short period and then we die) are, in the grand scheme of things, very, very, very tiny combinations of chemicals, the origins and original formation of which are also subject to wonder.

Now, with that intimidating background to be constantly remembered, we are almost ready to begin our metaphysical search for some ultimate truths. First, however, based upon those little bits of knowledge we have about the universe, we must make some reasonable assumptions.

Assumption #1 is that somewhere out there in those 100 billion galaxies there are numerous stars which, like our sun, have orbiting planets that are somewhat similar to the Earth. Not necessarily exactly like the Earth in either climate or chemical composition, but planets containing water and carbon and nitrogen and all the stuff required to support living organisms here on earth.

Assumption #2 is that, among all those trillions of solar systems, there are living organisms on some of those earth-like planets.

Assumption #3 is that some of those living organisms on some of those planets have significantly greater knowledge than we have regarding the physical sciences and math.

Assumption #4 is that some of those smarter organisms from some other galaxy, or maybe even from our own galaxy, are probably going to figure out how they can get to here from there before we figure out how we can get to there from here. In fact, some of "them" from way out elsewhere may have already been here and looked around. Some people believe that. It could even be that after they assessed our circumstances, they decided they were not interested in staying because they concluded that we humans have already screwed things up here so bad.

Finally, Assumption #5 is that the Laws of Physics that science relies upon here on the Earth operate in a consistent manner throughout the physical universe.

Even the tiny bits of knowledge now known by the astronomers, combined with Assumptions #1 thru #4, invite almost endless questions – questions of both a physical nature and a spiritual nature. There are correct answers to all of these questions. During our lives, however, we will probably not know any of them. However, we can ask the questions and we can wonder and speculate about what the answers might be.

So, to begin, we return to what seem to be the most basic questions. Where did all the stuff in the universe come from? How did the gases that make up the stars and the water and other basic chemical materials that make up the planets and the moons and comets and assorted "space junk" come to be? And how did the stars and planets form into spheres and how did they get to where they are? And why do most of them spin? And why is there a gravitational force that causes separate masses of matter to be attracted to one another? Who or what could ever think that "gravity" rule up?

As we ponder those questions, there arise others even more fundamental. For example, why do we assume there is only one universe? Even the word "universe" denotes a singularity. Where does the universe we know of end? Or is it infinite in size? Is there anything, even empty space, outside of the defined universe? And if there is empty space beyond our universe, what do we call that space? Could there be another universe out there in that space, and, if so, is it controlled by different laws of physics? And, if there could be one more universe, why could there not be two or three more? Could there even be a million more?

Finally, here is one more intriguing question: Could there be a parallel universe of another kind that occupies a different dimension of the same space we occupy on Earth? And could that explain the "supernatural" events, such as the appearance of spirits and the occurrence of "miracles," that many humans have claimed to have witnessed throughout the centuries? And to double back to the beginning, if there is only one universe, why is that so?

The scientific answers to those questions are not known yet by anyone who occupies the same dimensions on this planet that we occupy. Answers suggested by faith-based religions do not provide any comfort. The defining tenants of organized religions have been made up along the way and modified as needed to keep the flocks under control when science thoroughly discredited a previous belief, such as the belief that the earth is flat.

In case you haven't noticed, we have moved to a discussion of the spiritual side of things galactic. In fact, the spiritual and the physical aspects of this subject become, in some respects, inseparable at this point. Remember that we are assuming that there are intelligent creatures living out there on some of the millions or billions of planets in our universe. I wonder how long these other intelligent creatures live, and whether they experience physical death in a manner similar to us, and I wonder what they know or what they think they know about God and creation and the possibility of a spiritual life at any level. If we, who live and die on the Earth, do continue to exist in a spiritual form (or in any other form) after our physical lives end, and if we have a heaven to go to, as many of us believe, then fairness dictates that same opportunity should apply to every race of intelligent creatures in every other galaxy. So do they have a heaven? And if they do, is it the same one as ours and where is it? And by the way, where is ours? Is heaven even a place at all, or could it be just an alternate state of being? Isn't everything that exists required to be somewhere? Maybe each galaxy has its own separate heaven. Think about that…100 billion different heavens. Wow!! Maybe the 100 billion different heavens combine to make up a different universe of heavens. Maybe a heaven is a physical place, or maybe not. And maybe heaven doesn't exist at all. That creates quite a spread of possibilities – from 100 billion heavens to zero heavens. And, if it's alright, I have one more question about heaven. What if there is some kind of spiritual life after death, but there **ISN'T** any heaven for our spirits to occupy? What then?

And finally, we might as well discuss the elephant in the room. What about God? Does God even exist? And if there is a God – a Supreme Being – do any of those alien guys who live in one of those other galaxies know for sure? And if they do, how did they obtain that information? And here are some more good questions: Does God, if there is one, have a gender? Is there a different God in charge of each Galaxy or is there just one? I would vote for the "just one" answer, but the universe is a really big place for just one God to manage, even if he is the "One and Only" God. It seems like the first thing an eternally existing God would do is create some company for himself. But how can something happen "first" to God if he has always existed?

You can believe whatever you choose and attend whatever church you want to attend or attend none at all. I, for one, find it impossible to conclude that this universe and everything in it and the way it works is one very big and complex accident. For instance, consider the laws of physics. We are told by scientists that the laws of physics apply everywhere in the universe. And they have actually used those laws of physics to send astronauts successfully to the moon and back. They also have sent electronic and nuclear powered rovers to Mars and recorded the data those rovers transmitted back to them here on the earth. So they must be right about the constancy of the laws of physics throughout the known universe.

There are hundreds of laws of physics that apply to motion and mass and electricity and gravity and on and on. That can't all be accidental, can it? It seems to me that somebody a lot smarter than us had to be in charge of devising and integrating and coordinating all those laws of physics and putting them into operation in the appropriate sequence. It would take a pretty powerful and intelligent dude to do all that.

So those are the reasons I conclude there is a Supreme Being. And it's okay with me if some call this spiritual power "God." It is as good a name as any other and easy to pronounce. But that isn't the end of it. Even if the Supreme Being that I believe must exist does, in fact, exist, then equally tough questions arise. Does that mean that we humans, or any of the intelligent creatures in other places in the universe, are guaranteed some kind of spiritual existence after our physical death? And, by the way, how can this god be described and what comes next in what seems to be an imperfectly phased creation of this universe? In other words, after all the experiences, the successes, the failures, the victories, the tragedies, the education and the thought, what do we believe ABOUT this creator-force called "God" and about the significance, if any, of individual humans in the eyes of that "God," and why?

II. <u>Credo</u>

There must exist in some dimension an intelligent spiritual force that conceived of the universe, in all its complexity, and then acted as the "First Mover" or "Creator" to initiate the process by which that universe has developed into what it has become. And that First Mover (or a buddy with similar extraordinary powers) had to create the combination of energies and materials for, and also foresee, initiate and predestine the "Big Bang" process by which the one universe, as we presently know it, began its existence and developed.

Such things do not happen, nay, COULD NOT HAPPEN, without a Catalyst. And in this case, that Catalyst had to combine measures of power and intelligence beyond the combined abilities of all of the scientific geniuses who have ever lived or will live in the future. And having assembled the necessary materials, the next step was equally unimaginable and complex – that was, to bring into existence and prevent the interaction of the forces required to place and keep those materials under the enormous pressures required to initiate an explosion that would result in the formation and expansion of 100 billion galaxies with energy so sustained that it is still dispersing today, 4.2 Billion years later.

Unless you are willing to ignore all the science, there is only one explanation for the locations and continued dynamics of the 100 billion galaxies. And that body of science is solid. It was accomplished through calculations by the likes of Einstein that have been tested and re-tested. They are based upon known and confirmed scientific data, much of it competitively gathered during the NASA space exploration projects during the second half of the 20th century. We would be fools to ignore such consistent scientific proof – There WAS a "Big Bang," and we, the human race on this little planet orbiting about 270 Million miles from an insignificant star, are in existence as a result of that Big Bang. And for the reasons set forth above, imagine the "Big Bang" could not have occurred at all and would not have been explainable within our level of understanding, without the participation of a "First Mover."

And still, the question remains: Where did all the materials come from? It does not require the brain of a genius to recognize that not one atom of the complex physical matter that comprises the universe, whether liquid, gas or solid, could be a part of our present universe unless it was either already in existence for, or created as part of, the Big Bang. To begin with, if there is no Creator, then where did all this material which is composed of many different chemicals that form solids and liquids and gases come from? Logic requires a Creator. However, that is where my agreements with religious teachings about the nature and attitude of God end.

I do not believe in a God who exercises daily control of events of the creatures in this universe. There may be other universes where he does, but I believe that absolutely every physical development and event that has occurred and that will occur in the future with respect to the size, composition and behavior of the universe, down to the smallest piece of space junk, has been predetermined by the Big Bang. From the moment the Big Bang occurred, and maybe even long before that, it was "hands off" from the First Mover. All of the materials, all of the rules of physics, every aspect of creation and development of this universe, were complete.

In short, I do not believe that anything integral to the creation and development of this physical universe or the living organisms that occupy it was, is or will be "accidental" or a "matter of chance." "Time," as we know and conceive it, began at that moment and from then until now the Creator/First Mover we call "God" has done nothing to modify in any way any of the "program" he embedded in that "Big Bang" that brought about the universe, the galaxies, the solar systems and, eventually, this planet and the living organisms that have come to occupy it. And because that is my belief regarding God's non-intervention in the development of the universe, that same non-intervention must logically be his practice as to all living organisms that occupy any other planet in this universe.

The foregoing, combined with some of my personal experiences, lead next to the conclusion that, except for the possible analgesic effect upon the psyche of the person doing it, prayer is a useless exercise. There is no "power" in prayer. We are the victims and the beneficiaries, as the case may be, of our own fortuitous circumstance and our own choices and conduct. We have been left by the Creator to our own devices. We must uncover and apply our knowledge of the universe, learn to deal with the tragedies, problems, afflictions and good and bad fortunes that life visits upon us, and generally make our own way in our own times on this earth. Praying to him for help never ever works because he is not listening.

Look beyond your own surroundings to other parts of this world; consider the brutal experiences of the human race just during the short period that human history has been recorded. If you do that, you can only conclude that, despite all of the praying and supplication and tithing and sacrifice offered at the alters built for God, nevertheless, all humans, from the first to those here now, have endured various diseases, personal and natural tragedies, the consequences of wars and injustice and other terrible burdens, sometimes from birth to death. Prayer has never had any impact on any of that.

Now, what about God? Who or what is God? My own guess is that God is neither good nor bad. Nor is God male or female. Custom has chosen to apply masculine pronouns in our references to this First Mover. There can be little doubt that the masculine references are a product of male dominance in earlier times when brawn was more essential to survival than brain power.

Many religions teach that we are "created in his likeness." In other words, they claim we humans look like him. But who knows what a spirit looks like? In fact, we can't know. For that matter, how can a spirit look like anything at all? And who decided that God intends to sit in judgment of each of us after we die? Why would he even bother if he already knows everything? Nope. I just can't swallow that judgment day stuff.

However, I know that in recent years I have had two very strange experiences following the deaths of two loved ones that cannot be explained without attributing some activity to an unseen, unknown source. And because of those experiences, I willingly concede the possibility of some kind of continued existence after physical death. But for those personal experiences, I would not have any hope of such a possibility. The most fascinating aspect to this question of whether there is a continuing existence after physical death is that we will only know the answer if and when we find ourselves in another dimension. If there is nothing on the other side of this physical life, we will never know it.

In the final analysis, as we pass through this life, we each govern ourselves, select and manage our own relationships, and decide whether we will behave like Hitler or like Mother Teresa, or somewhere in between. The Creator instilled in each of us the ability to distinguish between (on the one hand) behavior that is consistent with the peaceful and just conduct of our affairs and (on the other hand) behavior that is unjust, dishonest or otherwise harmful to the common good.

Somewhere, somehow, we are programmed to know that life is mostly about our relationships with ourselves and others. And like our "lower animal" brethren, We KNOW by the time we are mature what conduct is "good" and what conduct is "bad." We KNOW how to organize societies to control harmful behavior and to promote the general welfare. And because that is the case, we have various forms of government around our planet.

The primary responsibilities of any government are to regulate behavior for the common safety and to protect its citizens from harm. Some governments meet these responsibilities and some do not. Some are corrupt, some are aggressive, some are evil to the core, but they are all composed of people who KNOW that their motives are either in the interest of the common good or not. Are the intelligent organisms in other galaxies all the same in that respect? Maybe there is a society somewhere that requires no central legal authority to assure mutual respect and fair treatment among its members.

Scientists tell us that we who now occupy the earth constitute approximately the Four-Hundredth generation of the human species. As best I can tell, the Creator had no contract with any of those generations assuring that each human would be a perfect specimen, incapable of corrupt, or self-serving, or aggressive or evil behavior. Nor was the Creator obligated to bring forth the human species at all. There will always be evil people and people of ill will among us. It is for us, not for God, to define, control and minimize "bad" behavior of all sorts while we inhabit this planet. Likewise, God owes us no obligation to punish the bad actors after physical death eliminates them from our midst, nor does God have any obligation to provide a spiritual after-life for anybody, much less a spiritual after-life involving "everlasting life" in luxurious accommodations. What I can say with certainty is that there either IS or there IS NOT a spiritual afterlife that awaits us; and there is absolutely nothing we can do about it, either way,

However, I do believe that there is a spiritual existence that follows physical death. We must face the reality that human life either entirely ceases in all respects upon physical death and, therefore, has no meaning at all, or is about something. For basically the same reasons that I do not believe the creation of the universe was accidental, I do not believe the creation of intelligent human life was accidental. It defies reason to conclude that creatures that have the capacity to distinguish between good and evil have no purpose in the scope of creation except to exist for a very short time span and then die. Therefore, I believe a life of relative kindness to others has positive consequences after death, and that a life of evil behavior impacting the lives of others brings negative consequences. But I don't pretend to know what either might be.

Nor do I believe that God has any inclination to intervene in the affairs of this planet, whether global or personal. Sorry to break the news, but God is not a sports fan. He will not cause an errant forward pass, he will not give a goalkeeper special powers or cause a third baseman to hit a home run if he crosses himself as he steps into the batter's box.

Very bad things happen to people all around the earth every day. There are natural disasters like floods, earthquakes, tornados, droughts and tragedies like wars, human cruelty, diseases, epidemics, accidents, birth defects. And every living creature on this planet is required, at some point, to die. Some among us die as babies and some die as young adults and some of us live longer. What is fair about that? There are naysayers who legitimately complain about such matters, and they say if God is so smart and powerful, why didn't he put us and our planet together so our bodies always work right and do right and so we don't have natural events and accidents that hurt or kill us? Why did he put us here without at least a basic operations manual?

Nevertheless, with 100 billion galaxies in our universe, we who find ourselves anchored to this place we call "Earth" are entitled to stare out into space in awe and to be confused. We are simply adrift somewhere in the galaxy we call the "Milky Way" with no map, no operating manual and plenty to wonder about. Our only reliable governors are the laws of physics, and even they may not be permanent. If God turned them on with the Big Bang, I guess he can turn them off.

Maybe he put one of those operations manuals on some other planet in some other galaxy. Or maybe some of those organisms who live in another galaxy have figured it all out. Maybe they don't even age and die like we do. Maybe. But if they don't die like we do, what is fair about that? Oh. Wait. Who ever said God had to be fair to everybody he created in all 100 billion galaxies?

Right now, my brain hurts. It is going to rest for a while. But there are abundant additional questions left to wonder about. Such as this. Give me one good reason why, out of all of the millions of planets in each of the 100 billion galaxies, why would God send his "only begotten son" to this planet, and allow that son's human life to be violently sacrificed for the likes of us when we can't even get along with one another? Just asking.

<u>Love</u>

ERNEST HEMINGWAY said this: "When two people love one another, there can be no good end to it." Truer words have never been written. But that is not the entire story of mutual love. There is, remember, all the time between that first day when two people experience the kind of love that possesses and dominates a person's entire being, body and soul, and the day love dies, no matter how or when that last day arrives. Those are the days we are most alive.

I am pretty good with words. But there are none in my lexicon to fairly describe romantic love. Romance flies with the wind in one moment and struggles to survive through pain and tears in others, while its owners cling together instead of running away.

There is, however, yet another kind of love, the strength and intimacy of which is most often lifelong and unsurpassed. I am a father and I love all my children and their children, but I cannot even presume to imagine the depth of a mother's love for her child. There is, I believe, nothing in God's creation so unconditional and there is nothing that compares to the lasting emotional pain a mother endures when Death claims her child.

To be willing to love is to have the courage to risk its premature loss. Nevertheless, both romantic love and parental love are, for most of us, the most essential components of living. And during those days between the beginning and the end of each kind of love, there is the essence of life. Where there is love, there is a continuing mutual tenderness, a tolerance, an understanding, a oneness in being and in spirit that can never be duplicated, all of which defy further description. These are the qualities of life that render bearable the often anguishing challenges that fate brings to all of us. For no matter what you perceive on the surface, everyone hides their greatest wounds from most of the rest of the world.

Few of us could survive long in this phase of existence, nor would we have the desire to do so, if we could not love somebody and feel the love of someone for us. We are that dependent upon love, and thus should always be willing to take the risk and to pay the price.

The love of two people, one for another, whether romantic or parental, is, as Hemingway said, destined to a painful end, no matter the cause. But the pain of the loss is justified by the wonder of the experience while it lasts. Take it from a man who has been there and back.

Dear Reader,

We have reached the point, dear reader, when it is time for me to end this book and enjoy a glass of wine, because, as least for the moment, I have told you almost everything I know.

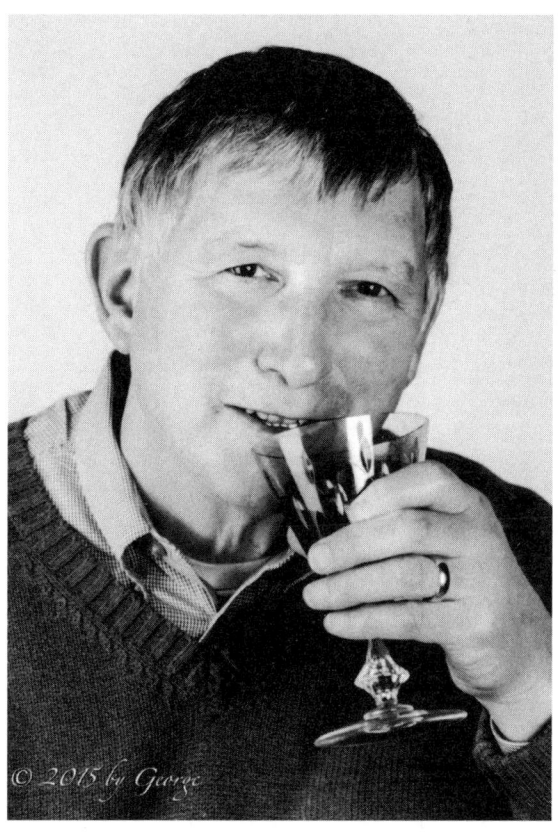

David Miller

ABOUT THE AUTHOR

The author lives in southern Indiana. This book provides anecdotal evidence that there are some people remaining in Indiana who can think and write. The author is also an attorney who is proud of his profession. However, he believes this book is necessary to demonstrate that some attorneys are actual compassionate human beings who laugh, cry, love their children, wonder about the same things as other people, and admit they don't know everything. The author is also a member of Sam's Club and a personal friend of several greeters there, all of whom have urged him to never retire.

ABOUT THIS BOOK

Many curious friends who heard I was working on this book have recently asked me: "What's your book about?" I just told them I was pleased that they asked, but that would remain my secret until they bought the book and read it. It wasn't a fair question anyway. If you read the "Introduction" you will understand why.